IS-31.A: Mitigation eGrants
for the Grant Applicant
By

Fema

10/31/2013

IS-31: Mitigation eGrants for the Grant Applicant

Table of Contents:

Lesson 1: What is eGrants?

Lesson Overview

Upon completion of this lesson, you should be able to:

- Explain the function of eGrants
- Identify eGrants users
- Describe the eGrants application process

eGrants System

The Federal Emergency Management Agency's eGrants system was developed to provide State and Territorial governments, Federally-recognized Indian Tribal governments, and local governments with the ability to apply for and manage their grant and subgrant application processes electronically.

Specifically, eGrants functions include:

- The creation and submission of pre-applications to State, Territory, and Federally-recognized Indian Tribal government officials
- The creation and submission of subgrant applications to State, Territory, and Federally-recognized Indian Tribal government officials
- The review and processing of subgrant applications
- The creation and submission of grant applications to FEMA
- The review and processing of grant awards
- The quarterly reporting of performance and financial status to FEMA of grants awarded by FEMA

eGrants Users

The people who use the eGrants system are:

- State and U.S. Territory officials
- Subgrant applicants (State-level agencies; Federally-recognized Indian Tribal governments; local governments, including State-recognized tribes, authorized Tribal organizations, and Alaska Native villages)
- Local government officials, including State-recognized tribes, authorized Tribal organizations, and Alaska Native villages
- FEMA

There are two major categories of applicants who use the eGrants system:

1. Grant applicants (State, Territory, and/or Federally-recognized Indian Tribal government officials)
2. Subgrant applicants (Local, and/or Indian Federally-recognized Tribal government officials)

This course focuses on the eGrants system for grant applicants.

Subgrant & Grant Applicants

eGrants allows subgrant applicants to:

- Create and submit pre-applications to the grant applicant
- Create and submit subgrant applications
- Revise and resubmit subgrant applications

eGrants allows grant applicants to:

- Process paper-intake subgrant applications (Process paper subgrant applications, Application Intake)
- Review subgrant applications
- Create and submit a grant as subgrant application
- Create and submit a grant application to FEMA
- Review and process grant applications
- Review and accept/not accept award packages
- Prepare and submit quarterly reports

Grant Types

FEMA currently offers four types of mitigation grants.

Pre-Disaster Mitigation (PDM) program icon —Funding for the PDM program is provided to assist State, local, and Tribal governments in implementing cost-effective hazard mitigation activities.

Flood Mitigation Assistance (FMA) program icon —FMA was created to reduce or eliminate claims under the National Flood Insurance Program (NFIP). FMA grants are available through eGrants. FMA provides funding to assist communities in implementing measures to reduce or eliminate long-term risk of flood damage.

Severe Repetitive Loss (SRL) program icon —This program provides financial assistance to States and communities to mitigate flood damage to severe-repetitive-loss properties and to reduce losses to the National Flood Insurance Fund from claims relating to such properties.

Repetitive Flood Claims (RFC) program icon —This program provides financial assistance to States and communities to reduce flood damages to insured properties that have had one or more claims to NFIP.

Currently, eGrants provides an online application and grants management system for PDM, FMA, SRL and RFC only.

The Application Process

The application process in eGrants follows a specific workflow sequence. Initially, a local official creates a subgrant application and submits it to the appropriate grant applicant for review. A subgrant application can be created in one of several ways:

- Directly by the subgrant applicant in eGrants
- Submitted as a paper subgrant application and entered into eGrants by the grant applicant

The grant applicant can also create subgrant applications that are included in the grant application. These are called grant as subgrant applications.

Next, a grant applicant official reviews the subgrant application. He or she may request revisions. If revisions are requested, the local official may revise the subgrant application and resubmit it. Once the subgrant application is reviewed and complete, the grant applicant may include it in a larger grant application that is submitted to FEMA. FEMA then reviews the grant application and either approves it, disapproves it, or requests revisions.

Lesson Summary

In this lesson, you learned about the:

- The function of eGrants
- eGrants users
- eGrants application process

Some key points from this lesson:

- eGrants allows users to create, submit, review, and process subgrant and grant applications.
- At this time, FMA, PDM, SRL, and RFC grants can be processed using eGrants
- eGrants is designed for use by FEMA and State, Territory, Tribal, and local government officials.
- The eGrants process involves the creation and submission of a subgrant application to the grant applicant. The grant applicant may then include that subgrant application in the larger grant application submitted to FEMA.

Lesson 2: Logging in to and out of eGrants

Lesson Overview

Upon completion of this lesson, you should be able to:

- Explain the registration procedure for eGrants
- Access the Integrated Security and Access Control System (ISAACS)
- Register for ISAACS
- Create a User ID
- Create a Password
- Request access to Mitigation eGrants
- Log in to eGrants
- Log out of eGrants

Scenario

State Official: Steve Miller

Community: State of Florida

Problem: Steve has been given the task of managing FEMA mitigation grant applications.

Next Step: Steve will need to create a new eGrants user account.

Audio Transcript: Hi, I'm Steve Miller. I work for the Florida Emergency Management Agency. My new assignment is to manage FEMA mitigation grant applications. I will need to set up a new account and learn my way around the eGrants system. Let's get started!

(Audio Transcript)

Hi, I'm Steve Miller. I work for the Florida Emergency Management Agency. My new assignment is to manage FEMA mitigation grant applications. I will need to set up a new account and learn my way around the eGrants system. Let's get started!

eGrants Access

Only registered users may access FEMA's eGrants system. Because eGrants is a Web-based system, users' computers must meet some minimum system requirements. For eGrants, a computer must have:

- Microsoft Internet Explorer, version 5.0 or better with 128-bit encryption, or
- Netscape, version 4.7 or better with 128-bit encryption, and
- Access to an e-mail service

After ensuring that the above requirements are met, users may begin the registration process.

Registration Process

The registration process occurs only the first time a user attempts to access eGrants. This process involves four steps:

1. Contact the FEMA Regional Office to receive an Access ID. This step prevents unauthorized individuals from clogging the system with bogus User ID requests.
2. Use the Department of Homeland Security (DHS) Integrated Security and Access Control System (ISAACS) registration screens to create an account.
3. Once the account has been created, request access to Mitigation eGrants. A FEMA official will approve or reject this request. If the request is rejected, the individual will not be permitted to access eGrants.
4. If the request is approved, an e-mail notification is sent notifying you that you are authorized to access Mitigation eGrants.

eGrants

eGrants is a Web-based system; you must access it via a URL in a browser.

1. Open your browser.
2. Type in the eGrants URL: https://portal.fema.gov
3. If you have an existing ISAACS account, type in your User ID and Password. If you do not have an account, you will need to create one.

NOTE: Bookmark this site to avoid having to re-type the URL.

New Users

A grant applicant logging in to eGrants for the first time will need to create an account in the DHS ISAACS system by selecting the **New User?** button.

Security Question

To begin the registration process, the grant applicant should complete the security check question by entering into the text box the letters shown in the graphic and selecting the **Submit** button.

This will help protect your information from automated attacks.

NOTE: The graphic generated on this page is just an example. The graphic you receive will be different.

User ID

During the registration process, each grant applicant will create a unique User Identification (ID). This ID should be something you can remember, and must also meet the following criteria (check with FEMA to learn of any required naming conventions for your area):

- All ID letters must be lower case.
- The ID must have a minimum of 7 characters.
- The ID cannot exceed a maximum of 14 characters.
- The ID must not contain any special characters (e.g., %, $, or ?).

Locating an Organization's Name

During the registration process, each grant applicant will be asked to identify his or her organization name. It is important to ensure that everyone within the same organization inputs the name consistently.

To guarantee that this happens, rather than typing in the organization name, grant applicants should search the system to find the name as it already appears. In this case, the organization name we are searching for is "Florida Emergency Management Agency." Rather than typing it in, we will perform an organization search to ensure consistency.

(Show Me Simulation Transcript)

To begin the organization search, select the **SEARCH** link next to the **Organization** field from the Profile screen.

From the Organization Search screen, select the **Fiel**d drop-down menu.

The Field drop-down menu has three options – Contains, Starts with or Ends with. For this scenario, select the "Starts with" item.

Enter the search criteria into the Criteria field. In this case, the search criteria is "Florida".

Select the **SEARCH** button.

Select the organization from the search results. For this scenario, select the **Florida Emergency Management Agency** link from the Search Result list.

Note that your selection appears in the **Organization** field.

Password

During the registration process, you will create a unique Password in addition to your User ID. This Password, as well as being something you can remember, must meet the following criteria:

- The Password must contain a minimum of eight characters.
- Maximum of 14 characters
- The Password may not contain special characters (e.g., #, @, periods, or spaces).

For security reasons, it is recommended that you change your Password every 30 to 90 days.

NOTE: If you believe your Password has been compromised, immediately notify FEMA.

Account Created

Once you have completed all of the fields in the Registration Form and created a User ID and a Password, your account will be created. You will then need to request privileges for access to eGrants by selecting the link provided.

Requesting Access

Creating a DHS ISAACS account does not automatically generate access to eGrants. You need to request access to the Mitigations eGrants Application.

Select the "click here to request new privileges" link. Select the **Request Access** button under Mitigations eGrants Application.

To complete the request, you should type the Access ID in the appropriate field and select the **Submit** button. The Access ID is necessary to officially register to use eGrants. This is the Access ID you should have obtained from FEMA before starting the registration process.

NOTE: If, after your DHS ISAACS account has been created, you do not request privileges, you can log in at another time using the User ID and Password you created and request privileges.

Approval

The final step in a successful registration process involves receiving an e-mail from the FEMA Regional Office. If your request is approved, an e-mail will be sent that contains approval to access the eGrants system, and that may include information about the specific role assigned to you.

Role Options:

- **View/Print:** This role means that the applicant will have the ability to view and print applications in eGrants.
- **Create/Edit:** This role means that the applicant will have the ability to create, update, and make changes in eGrants.
- **Sign/Submit:** This role means that the applicant will have the ability to sign and submit applications in eGrants.

NOTE: FEMA will approve grant applicant user roles based on authorization given to FEMA by the grant applicant agency. Only those users that are authorized or officially delegated signature authority will receive the sign/submit role in eGrants.

NOTE: The e-mail does not come immediately. If no e-mail has been received, it means either that the registration has not yet been reviewed or that the user was not approved. You may contact your FEMA Regional Office to check the status of your registration.

Variations in Access Levels for Grant Applicants

When subgrant applicants are given access to eGrants, they are given View/Print, Create/Edit, and/or Sign/Submit access. For grant applicants, there are many more variations to the levels of access.

Grant applicants can be assigned a combination of different roles for the FMA/SRL/RFC and PDM grant types. For each of the grant types, grant users can be given View/Print, Create/Edit, and/or Sign/Submit access for:

- Applications
- Award Packages
- Quarterly Report Packages
- Financial Status Reports
- Performance Reports

An applicant's access levels for FMA, SRL, and RFC grants are the same, but the applicant's access level for PDM grants can differ from access levels for FMA, SRL, and RFC. For example, a grant applicant can have Sign/Submit access for FMA, SRL, and RFC grant applications, but have only View/Print access for PDM applications.

NOTE: If a user's access levels require updating, then FEMA can revise the approval based on authorization given to FEMA by the grant applicant agency. An e-mail will be sent to the user whenever changes are made to their approved access levels.

Logging In

After receiving approval from FEMA, grant applicants may access the eGrants system. The first screen will ask for a User ID and Password. In Steve's case, he completed the registration process, received e-mail confirmation from FEMA, and is now ready to log in to eGrants.

(Show Me Simulation Transcript)

To log in to FEMA's eGrants system, first select the **User ID** field. Next , type in the username. For this scenario, use Steve's User ID: steve_miller.

Click in the **Password** field and type in the password. For security reasons, the actual password is hidden as you type.

Select the **Login** button.

When you log in to eGrants, the Grant Applicant Homepage is displayed.

Logging Out

The eGrants system currently offers four of FEMA's mitigation grants.

Correct: The proper way to exit eGrants is to select the **Logout** Button or link located at the bottom or the top of the various eGrants screens. This will end the eGrants session.

Incorrect: The wrong way to exit eGrants is to select the **X** Button in the upper right corner of the browser. While this will close the eGrants window, it will not necessarily end the eGrants session **or** save data entered on the current screen.

Lesson Summary

In this lesson, you learned about the:

- Registration procedure for eGrants and ISAACS
- Access to Mitigation eGrants
- Log in to and out of eGrants

Some key points from this lesson:

- The registration procedure for eGrants includes receiving an Access ID, creating a User ID, creating a Password, searching for the appropriate organization, requesting access to Mitigation eGrants, and receiving approval.
- To access eGrants, applicants should type the URL into the address bar of a browser that meets the requirements.
- To register for eGrants, applicants should contact the appropriate FEMA Regional Office for an Access ID and create an account in DHS ISAACS.
- User IDs must be between seven and 14 characters long and contain no special characters. For some FEMA Regions, User IDs must follow specified naming conventions.
- Passwords must be between eight and 14 characters in length and contain no special characters.
- A User ID and a Password are required to log in to eGrants.
- To log out of eGrants, applicants must select the **Logout** button or the **Logout** link.

Lesson 3: Navigating within eGrants

Lesson Overview

Upon completion of this lesson, you should be able to:

- Navigate within the eGrants system
- Access eGrants system help links
- Change a User Profile
- Change a Password
- Retrieve a forgotten Password

Scenario

State Official: Steve Miller

Community: State of Florida

Problem: Steve has been given the task of managing, FEMA grant applications for his state.

To Date: Steve has registered for an ISAACS account, requested and has been approved for Mitigation eGrants access.

Next Step: Steve will need to become familiar with how to navigate in eGrants.

(Audio Transcript)

Hi, I'm Steve. I work for the State of Florida. I will be managing and reviewing subgrant applications and creating and completing FEMA mitigation grant applications. Right now, I've just logged in to eGrants for the first time, so I'll need to learn how to use the system before beginning to review any subgrant applications or creating a grant application.

Navigation Buttons

Navigation within eGrants is similar to navigation within other Web-based applications. Navigation features include links, buttons, scroll bars, etc.

Buttons: Users may select buttons to perform specific functions. Within eGrants, there are several buttons that appear throughout the system. Some button functions are:

Save: Stores data from the current screen into the eGrants system.

Save and Continue: Stores data from the current screen into the eGrants system and advances to the next screen.

Go Back: Returns to the previous screen

Attach File: Initiates selection of a file to be attached to the application

NOTE: If a button appears gray or dim, it is not active. This means that the function controlled by the button is not available at that time.

Input

Inputting information in eGrants is similar to inputting information in other Web-based applications.
There are two primary ways to input data in eGrants:

Drop-down List: These fields offer users the opportunity to select an item from a limited list. To do so, select the arrow at the right of the field to see the list. Then, to choose the most appropriate option, simply select that item from the menu.

Text Fields: These fields offer users the opportunity to input data by typing. Simply place the cursor at the beginning of the field and use the keyboard to type the appropriate information. If the data must be entered in a specific format, an example of that format will be shown next to the text field in eGrants.

NOTE: Certain fields within each section of the subgrant application are required and must be completed. These fields are designated by red asterisks (*). While eGrants allows required fields to be passed over within each section, the subgrant application cannot be successfully submitted until all required fields in every section are complete.

Scrolling

Another navigation feature in eGrants is the Scroll Bar. On occasion, the screen will be longer than the available window space. In order to see the lower portion of the screen, users must scroll down. The Scroll Bar is located along the right edge of any screen that requires scrolling.

A user may simply move his/her cursor to the arrow at either the top or the bottom of the Scroll Bar to see the appropriate portion of the screen.

Hyperlinks

Another navigation feature in eGrants is the Hyperlink. A Hyperlink is displayed as blue underlined text. In eGrants, a Hyperlink opens a new window so that the user may view the additional information while maintaining his or her location in eGrants.

Steve is curious about the eGrants features and wishes to see what happens when he selects a Hyperlink.

To learn what a DUNS number is, select the **DUNS Number** hyperlink.

A new window opens with additional information. When you are finished reading the information, select the **Close** button to close the window.

Help Links

Another navigation feature in eGrants is the Help link. Help links appear to the right of a field as the word "Help" in blue underlined text. Selecting this link will produce a pop-up window with details about the information that is expected in that field.

Steve wishes to follow a Help link to see what type of information will appear.

Main Menu

There are three types of menus in eGrants. One menu is the **Main** menu, located across the bottom of the eGrants screen. The items in this menu allow applicants to access a variety of eGrants features:

FEMA Home: This feature moves the applicant to the FEMA Home Page.

eGrants Home: This feature moves the applicant to the Grant Applicant Home Page.

Contact Us: This feature opens a new window offering FEMA phone numbers and an online information request form.

Frequently Asked Questions: This feature opens a new window offering a list of common questions about eGrants, along with specific answers.

Glossary: This feature opens a new window offering an extensive, alphabetized list of eGrants terms and definitions.

Help: This feature opens a new window offering information, as well as definitions of technical concepts related to eGrants use.

Task Menu

Task menus such as those found on the Grant Applicant Home Page allow users to navigate to a particular task to perform.

In this example, users have five task options from which to choose.

Sidebar Menu

Sidebar menus appear on the left side of the application screen. This menu assists users in moving directly to a specific section of the subgrant application without having to view each section sequentially.

Changing a Profile

Over time, certain information may change, such as a telephone number or an e-mail address. If information that was entered during registration later changes, a user should update the information in the eGrants User Profile.

Steve wishes to update his phone number. It appears incorrectly as (727) 555-2560, and it should be (727) 555-4233.

There are four links in the top right-hand corner of the Applicant Homepage. To begin changing your profile, select the third link, the **Edit Profile link**.

The User Profile page appears with the current user's information filling in the fields. Scroll down until you find the field that you want to edit. To change the information:

- Select the field
- Delete the old information
- Input the new information

Select the **Submit button** to store the changes made.

After the changes are saved, a message appears saying, "Your profile has been updated. Thank you."

Changing a Password

It is your responsibility to secure and protect your Password from easy detection and use by unauthorized users. Remember, anyone with your User ID and Password can log in to eGrants as *you*, and the system cannot tell the difference.

As a precaution, you should change your Password every 30 to 90 days. Additionally, if you feel your Password has been compromised, you should change it.

Select the **Change Password** link on the Grant Applicant Home Page and input the current Password and the new Password.

Retrieving a Forgotten User ID or Password

If you have forgotten your User ID or Password, the eGrants system can e-mail you your User ID or a temporary Password.

To obtain your User ID, select the **Forgot User ID?** button on the DHS ISAACS login page. To retrieve a forgotten Password, select the **Forgot Pwd/PIN?** button. You will need to input your birthday and the e-mail address that is associated with your account. The User ID or temporary Password will be e-mailed to that e-mail address.

After you have logged in with a temporary Password, you will be prompted to change the temporary Password.

Save

To ensure that information entered in eGrants is successfully captured, users must always save their data. At the bottom of each page are two buttons to facilitate this process. Failure to use the Save Buttons will result in the loss of all data entered since the last time the application was saved.

Save and Continue: This feature saves the data entered in a section of the application and automatically moves the applicant to the next section.

Save: This feature saves the data entered in a section of the application, but does not automatically move the user to the next section.

NOTE: On some screens, a Go Back button will appear. This button will return you to the previous screen, but does not save the data from the current screen.

Data Loss

One concern while in eGrants is the potential loss of data. There are two main areas of risk. **Risk #1—Buttons:** Using the **Back** and **Next** buttons on the browser toolbar will result in data loss. Users should use only the **Save**, **Save and Continue**, and **Go Back** buttons within eGrants. The **Save**, **Save and Continue** buttons ensure that the information entered is saved and stored in eGrants.

Risk #2—Expiration: Each eGrants session expires after 30 minutes of inactivity. The time until expiration is displayed at the top of the eGrants screen. As the session nears expiration, a reminder screen will appear asking if the user wishes to continue the session. Selecting Continue returns the user to eGrants for a new 30-minute session. Lack of response closes the eGrants session and causes all unsaved data to be lost.

Lesson Summary

In this lesson, you learned to:

- Navigate within the eGrants system
- Access eGrants system help links
- Change a User Profile
- Change a Password
- Retrieve a forgotten Password

Some key points from this lesson:

- eGrants offers a variety of standard Web-based navigation features, including menus, scrolling, text fields, hyperlinks, and help links.
- Your Password should be changed every 30 to 90 days.
- If you have forgotten your Password, the eGrants system can send you a temporary Password.
- To avoid the loss of data, users should always use the **Save** or **Save and Continue** buttons at the end of each application screen.
- After 30 minutes of inactivity, eGrants will display a warning message. If the eGrants session is allowed to expire, all unsaved data will be lost.
- If a user's information changes, the User Profile should be updated.
- While required fields, marked with asterisks (*), may be skipped during information input, applications may not be submitted until all required fields are completed.

Lesson 4: eGrants for the Grant Applicants

Lesson Overview

Upon completion of this lesson, you should be able to:

- Describe the grant applicant's role in eGrants
- Set User preferences
- Manage User registrations

Grant Applicant Functions

In eGrants, grant applicants have three main roles: Administration, Applications, and Monitoring. Select each of these roles below to learn more.

NOTE: The Administrative function is discussed in this lesson. In Lessons 5 through 14, we will be discussing the Grant Applicants' application function. In Lesson 15, we will discuss the monitoring function.

In eGrants, grant applicants have three main functions: Administration; Applications, and Monitoring.

Administration: grant users may be assigned a role that allows them

1. To set the preferences for subgrant users and
2. To manage subgrant user registration requests.

Applications: Subgrant applications are created in eGrants in one of three ways:

1. Electronic submission through eGrants by local officials,
2. Paper applications from local officials entered into eGrants by the grant applicant (Application Intake), and
3. Grant as subgrant applications entered into eGrants by the grant applicant. Grant applicant acting as subgrant applications, or grant as subgrant applications, are created in cases where the grant applicant wants to submit a subgrant application for the grant applicant state/Tribe/territory's mitigation activities (e.g., mitigation planning or management costs).

The grant applicant must review subgrant applications from local officials whether they are submitted by local officials in eGrants or entered on the local official's behalf by the grant user (Application Intake).

Only approved subgrants and any grant as subgrant applications may be included in a grant application to FEMA.

Monitoring: After the grant application has gone through the FEMA review process, if it is approved, the grant applicant will need to review the award package and choose whether to accept or decline it. Grant users are also expected to monitor awarded subgrants and report quarterly performance and financial status.

System Administration Function

As a grant user, you may be assigned a user role that allows you to manage the user registration requests of your subgrant applicants and set certain preferences in eGrants that control what your subgrant applicant users can see and do.

You must perform these functions before your subgrant applicants can submit applications.

Another Administration function is the printing of blank applications. Blank applications can be printed and sent to subgrant applicants who do not have eGrants access.

Preferences

Preferences allow you to specify which additional features available in eGrants will be available to your subgrant applicant users.

The preferences you will set are:

- **Enable subgrant Pre-Application**—allows you to activate the subgrant project pre-application module, which requires subgrant applicants to complete and submit a pre-application for their proposed projects (pre-applications are not required for planning or management cost activities)
- **Enable subgrant view of SF-424**—allows a subgrant applicant to view the SF-424 Application for Federal Assistance
- **Enable subgrant Assurances and Certification**—allows you to activate the Assurances and Certification forms for subgrant applicants to complete as part of their applications
- **Enable External E-mail**—allows e-mail notifications to be sent to the subgrant applicants from eGrants. If this preference is not set first or if external e-mail is not enabled, no registration e-mails will be sent to registrants.

NOTE: The preferences you select apply to **_all_** of your subgrant users. Preferences may not be set for individual users.

Setting the Preferences

To set the preferences, just select the Administration link from the Grant Applicant Home Page.

Then select the **Set Preferences** button. Choose "Yes" or "No" for each preference and select the **Save and Continue** button to save your choices.

Managing User Registrations Overview

User registration is the process by which information is collected from each user about his or her identity, the organization with which he or she is associated, and how he or she can be contacted. The actions that the user can perform are also set.

All users who want access to eGrants must register and be approved by an approving organization:

- Grant applicants approve or deny registration requests from subgrant applicants.
- The FEMA Regional Office approves or denies registration requests from grant applicants.

You can choose to view all user registrations or user registrations that are:

- Pending
- Approved
- Denied/Revoked

Pending registrations are those access request forms that have been completed online and submitted by a new user, but have not yet been reviewed and approved or denied. If you have been assigned the user role to review and approve user registration requests from your subgrant applicants, you must review pending registrations and either approve or deny the registration requests.

NOTE: The requesting user cannot access eGrants until his or her registration request has been approved. eGrants does not automatically notify you of new registration requests, so you need to check for pending registrations on a regular basis.

NOTE: Subgrant applicants must use a different access ID than grant applicants. Contact the FEMA Regional Office to receive an access ID for your subgrant applicants.

Reviewing User Registrations

View—allows you to read the user registration information (by selecting the name of the user).

For each <u>pending registration</u> request, you may perform the following actions:

- **Review**—allows you to read the user registration information and select user role(s) or deny/revoke access to eGrants

For each <u>approved registration</u> request, you may perform the following actions:

- **Review**—allows you to read the user registration and change the selected role(s) or deny/revoke access

- **Reassign Permissions**—allows you to select and reassign permissions for applications that can be accessed by a particular user

For each <u>denied/revoked user registration,</u> you can perform the following action:

- **Review**—allows you to read the user registrations and approve the registration by selecting user role(s)

Approving and Denying User Registrations

User registrations can be accessed by selecting the **Administration** link from the Grant Applicant Home Page. Select the type of user registration you want to review from the sidebar menu. In addition to reviewing pending user registrations, you can review and modify approved and denied/revoked user registrations.

To approve a user registration, select the roles to be assigned to the user. Subgrant applicants are given View/Print, Create/Edit, and/or Sign/Submit access in eGrants. Grant applicants approve subgrant applicant user roles based on official authorization from the subgrant applicant. Only those users that are authorized or officially delegated signature authority by their organization should receive the sign/submit role in eGrants.

To deny a user registration, click on the **Deny/Revoke** checkbox and input text in the **Comments** text box explaining the reason for the denial of access.

After you have checked the appropriate box(es), click on the **Save and Continue** Button; a standard e-mail message advising the user of the denial or approval of his/her registration is displayed. You can modify/add to the e-mail text before sending it.

NOTE: If you want the user to be able to View/Print, Create/Edit, and Sign/Submit, you have to check all three boxes in the Action section. Just checking the Sign/Submit box will not provide Create/Edit privileges.

Changing User Roles

Sometimes it is necessary to change the roles a user is allowed to perform in eGrants—for example, a user may request permission to sign and submit subgrant applications in addition to being able to view/print and create/edit.

Roles are changed through the user registrations. You can search for the specific user for whom you are making the change by selecting the **All User Registrations** link in the sidebar menu and then selecting the **Search** button and inputting your search criteria.

NOTE: The **Search** function is available for searching through pending, approved, and denied/revoked user registrations.

Reassign User Permissions

Sometimes it is necessary to reassign permissions for applications that can be accessed by a particular user.

For example, if a subgrant user is retiring and needs to provide his/her successor with access to all of his/her applications, the subgrant user can use the reassign permissions function.

NOTE: FEMA can also reassign user permissions for grant applicants

NOTE: Be cautious when reassigning permissions. When you reassign permissions, you are reassigning access for **_all_** of the subgrant user's applications and it is irreversible.

Lesson Summary

- Grant applicants have three major roles in eGrants—Administration, Applications, and Monitoring.
- You may be assigned a user role that requires you to manage the user registration requests of subgrant applicants and set certain preferences in eGrants that control what your subgrant applicant users can see and do.
- Preferences allow you to specify which additional features available in eGrants will be available to your grant and subgrant applicant users.
- The preferences you select apply to all of your subgrant users. Preferences may not be set for individual users.
- All users who want access to eGrants must register and be approved by an approving organization. The requesting user cannot access eGrants until his or her registration request has been approved.
- Sometimes it is necessary to change the roles (actions) a user is allowed to perform within eGrants. Roles are changed through the user registrations.

Lesson 5: Subgrant Applications

Lesson Overview

Upon completion of this lesson, you should be able to:

- Describe the types of applications
- Describe the three methods of creating subgrant applications in eGrants
- Describe how to create subgrant applications
- Describe how to copy subgrant applications

Methods of Creating Subgrant Applications

As mentioned before, there are several methods for entering subgrant applications.

- **Entering Paper Subgrant Applications (Application Intake)**-Subgrant applications received by the grant applicant on paper may be entered by the grant user on behalf of the subgrant applicant. This application creates an electronic record of the subgrant application. The grant applicant must certify that a signed copy of the subgrant application is on file.
- **Subgrant Applications Submitted by Subgrant Applicants**-Subgrant applicants can submit subgrant applications to grant applicants in eGrants.
- **Grant Applicant Acting as Subgrant**-Grant applicants can also enter subgrant applications in eGrants (e.g., Management Costs Applications) that can be included in the grant application.

NOTE: Blank eGrants applications are available through the **Print Blank Application** link on both the Grant Applicant Home Page and the Subgrant Applicant Home Page, as well as on the FEMA Website. If subgrant applicants use the blank eGrants paper subgrant application, then entering these paper subgrant applications is much easier for the grant applicant.

Types of Applications

FEMA mitigation grant programs offer three types of subgrant applications:

- **Project Applications**-Project Applications are completed for any mitigation measure or activity proposed to reduce the risk of future damage, hardship, loss, or suffering. Typically, projects are "brick and mortar" construction or physical measures.
- **Planning Applications**-Planning Applications are completed for State, Tribal, local, or multi-jurisdictional mitigation planning activities that will result in a new or revised mitigation plan.
- **Management Cost Applications**-Management Cost Applications are completed for activities that are directly related to the administration of programs or promotion of

mitigation activities, and may include outreach and training, environmental/historic preservation reviews, developing applications, performing benefit/cost analyses, etc.

NOTE: Management Cost Applications are available _only_ for grant applicants. Grant applicants must complete a separate Management Cost Application to apply for their management costs. However, sub-applicant management cost activities, if necessary, are to be included in the sub-applicant's project or planning application.

It is important to know which application type is being proposed, because the sections required for each will vary. Additionally, depending on the type of subgrant application, the sections have different questions or different required fields.

Creating Applications

There are two methods you can use to create subgrant applications. You can choose to:

- **Create a New Application**-this option allows you to complete an entire blank application
- **Copy an Existing Application**-this option allows you to copy another application; you can choose to copy specific parts or the entire application

NOTE: The "copy an existing application" method is available only if the user has access to existing applications that can be copied.

(Show Me Simulation Transcript)

From the Grant Applicant Home Page, select the **Create New Subgrant Application** link.

On the Create New Grant as Subgrant Application screen, select the **Application Title** field and type in the title. In this scenario, use "Management Cost for Florida EMA."
Select the **Application Type** drop-down menu.

The **Application Type** drop-down menu has three options – Project Application, Planning Application, and Management Cost Application. For this scenario, select the "Management Cost Application" item.

Select the Save and Continue button.

On the Start New Subgrant Application screen, select the **Start New Application** button.

Copying an Application

When you choose to copy an existing application, the resulting application will be partly or completely filled with data from the previous one based on whether you choose to copy specific parts or the entire application.

Subgrant applications may be copied from one application type to another (e.g., project to planning); however, only the relevant sections will be available to copy. The **Copy Entire Application** function is available only if you are copying the same application type.

While Steve wishes to start with a blank application, he wants to learn how to copy one in case he needs to do so in the future.

(Show Me Simulation Transcript)

From the Grant Applicant Home Page screen, select the **Create New Subgrant Application** link.

On the Create New Grant as Subgrant Application screen, type in the title in the **Application title** field. In this case, use "Management Cost for Florida EMA".

Select the **Application Type** drop-down menu.

The **Application Type** drop-down menu has three options – Project Application, Planning Application, and Management Cost Application. For this scenario, select the "Management Cost Application" item.

Select the **Save and Continue** button.

On the Start New Subgrant Application screen, select the radio button in front of the application you wish to copy. For this scenario, select the 2012 Florida EMA Multi Hazard Mitigation Project application.

Select the **Copy Existing Application** button.

You will need to select the section(s) you want to copy. For some application types, you can copy the entire application by selecting the Entire Application check box. The Subapplicant, Contact, and Community sections are available for copying for all application types. In this case, you want to copy the Subapplicant, Contact, and Community sections.

Select the **Subapplicant** check box.

Select the **Contact** check box.

Select the **Community** check box.

Select the **Save and Continue** button.

You have created a new application by copying from an existing application.

Risks of Copying

When copying an existing grant or subgrant application, care must be taken to avoid the following:

- **Outdated information:** Since the original application was created in the past, some information on it may have changed. For example, contact information may have changed since the previous application was created. Also, the grant program guidelines may have changed.
- **Irrelevant Information:** While the original application may have been designed for a similar project, it is not safe to assume that all of the information in the old application will be appropriate for the new one.

It's always best to review every item in the application for accuracy prior to submission. Furthermore, it's a good idea to review the program regulations and guidance to ensure that all required and relevant information is provided in the applications.

Lesson Summary

In this lesson, you learned:

- the types of applications
- the three methods of creating subgrant applications in eGrants
- how to create subgrant applications
- how to copy subgrant applications

Some key points from this lesson:

- Subgrants can be created by subgrant applicants directly in eGrants, by grant applicants on behalf of local officials (Application Intake), and by grant applicants acting as subgrant applicants.
- Grant applicants must certify that they have a signed copy of the paper subgrant application for any subgrant applications entered into eGrants by the Application Intake method.
- There are three types of applications-Project, Planning, and Management Costs.
- Project Applications are completed for any mitigation measure or activity proposed to reduce the risk of future damage, hardship, loss, or suffering.
- Planning Applications are completed for State, Tribal, local, or multi-jurisdictional mitigation planning activities.
- Management Cost Applications are completed for activities that are directly related to the administration of programs or promotion of mitigation activities.
- Applications can be created either by creating a new application or by copying an existing application.
- When copying an existing application, be careful of outdated and/or irrelevant information.

Lesson 6: Entering Paper Subgrant Applications (Application Intake)

Lesson Overview

Upon completion of this lesson, you should be able to:

- Complete the Subapplication Section
- Describe how to complete the Contact Section
- Complete the Community section
- Complete the Mitigation Plan section
- Complete the Scope of Work section
- Describe how to complete the Properties section
- Complete the Cost Estimate section
- Complete the Cost Share section
- Describe how to complete the Cost Effectiveness section
- Identify the purpose of the Environmental/Historic Preservation section
- Identify the purpose of the Evaluation section
- Identify the purpose of the Assurances and Certifications section
- Complete the Comments and Attachments section

State Official: Steve Miller

Community: State of Florida

Problem: The State has received a paper subgrant application from the City of Adversity. The project application proposes to acquire and demolish 54 buildings along the Quake River that have experienced repetitive flooding.

Next Step: Steve will need to enter the paper subgrant application into eGrants.

Audio Transcript: We have just received a paper subgrant application from the City of Adversity. I will need to enter the paper subgrant application into eGrants on their behalf. I know that I'll have to complete several grant as subgrant applications for the state, and entering the paper subgrant application will be a good chance for me to learn about each of the sections of the subgrant application.

Entering a Paper Subgrant Application

Entering a paper subgrant application into eGrants is the same as entering a subgrant application, except the grant user has to certify that a signed copy of the paper subgrant application is on file. Let's help Steve enter the paper subgrant application. From the **Grant Applicant Home Page,** select the **Enter Paper Subgrant Application (Application Intake)** link. Enter "City of

Adversity Floodprone Property Acquisition" into the **Application Title field**. Select Project Application from Application Type drop-down menu.

You may enter a Paper Application Document Control Number if you have a document control system. In this case, the document control number is P-03-DE-FY07 and has already been entered. Enter your password into the **Password field.** In this case, enter in "grantapp." Check the electronic signature checkbox.

Enter "Luciana Rosa" in the **Signed by Field**. Enter "01-08-2008" in the **Date field**. Select the **Save and Continue button**.

Select the **Start New Application button**. The paper intake subgrant application has been created.

Application Sections

Each subgrant application contains numerous sections. Planning, Project, and Management Cost applications contain different section combinations. Also, remember that although some sections appear in several types of subgrants, those sections may look different in each of the types.

The application sections are available through a **Sidebar** menu similar to the one on this screen. The sections also appear in the main screen when a new application is created.

The simulations in this lesson will demonstrate how to complete some of these sections. Each simulation will begin on the screen that appears after the application section is selected from the sidebar menu.

After completing each section, remember to select the **Save and Continue** button so that your information isn't lost. Also, remember that every section must be complete before the application may be successfully submitted.

Applicant Information Section

The Applicant Information section appears for all application types. A complete Applicant Information section will contain detailed information about the organization requesting the subgrant. The information includes tax number, Congressional District, type of applicant, and non-profit status, if applicable. Some of these fields on the screen—those marked with asterisks (*)—are required, while the remainder are optional.

Help Steve enter the Applicant Information section. The appropriate information for the screen is provided on the paper application. The applicant in this case is the City of Adversity in Prosperity County.

In the Applicant Information section of the eGrants application, the **Name of Applicant**, the **State**, and the **Type of Applicant** are all required fields. For this example, assume that the

Applicant Information link has been selected and the organization Adversity has been located by use of the **Organization Search button**. At this point, the state field would automatically be populated. In this example, the state is "FL" (Florida).

The Applicant's Congressional District Number goes in the **Congressional District text field.** There is a hyperlink located next to the field to look up the Applicant's Congressional District.

Select the **Applicant Type drop-down menu** to choose the type of applicant completing the application. The available choices are "State Government," "Local Government," "Indian Tribal Government," "Special Governmental District," "Eligible Private Non-Profit," and "Other." In this example, we will choose "Local Government."

You can scroll down to complete the other fields of the Applicant Information section.

Contact Information Section

The Contact Information section collects information about whom to contact if there are questions about the application. The Contact Information section requires at least one point of contact (POC). Applicants must include the name of the POC, the agency, an address, phone number, and e-mail address. The address listed for the POC should be the address of the agency/organization that is applying for the FEMA funds.

An alternate POC is not required, but is suggested. Both the POC and the alternate POC may be notified via e-mail by the grant applicant regarding the status of the application once it has been submitted, if the external e-mail function is enabled in the grant user's preferences.

Community Information Section

The Community Information section collects information about the community that will benefit from the proposed mitigation activity.

Applicants should include information defining the community in the Community Profile field in this section. This information may include details such as descriptions of the general population, special populations, significant industries, businesses, and the geographic area.

Help Steve enter the Community Information section for the paper subgrant application. From the Sidebar menu, select the **Community Information link**.

From the Find Community page, you can search for the community by completing the **Community Name text field** or the **County Name text field.** You do not need to complete both, and you do not need to enter the full name of the community or county. eGrants can initiate a search using only a single letter, but that may produce an undesirably long list. For this example, we will search for the community of Adversity by typing "ADVER" into the **Community Name text field.**

You can choose to sort the results using a different criterion by selecting that criterion from the **Sort by drop-down menu**. The drop-down menu contains six options: "Community Name," "County Code," "CID Number," "CRS Community," "CRS Rating," and "U.S. Congressional District." For this example, we will choose to sort by "Community Name."

You can also choose the number of results to display per page by selecting the number in the **Results per page drop-down menu.** You can choose to display "5," "10," "15," or "20" results per page. For this example, we will choose to display 10 results per page.

Select the **Search button** to begin the search.

The search results are displayed. Select the radio button of the community you are searching for. In this example, you will select "Adversity, City of." The selected community appears on the Community Information section.

You can scroll down to complete the other fields of the Community Information section.

Mitigation Plan Information Section

The Mitigation Plan Information section allows the applicant to provide the status of the local and State/Tribal mitigation plans.

If there is a FEMA-approved plan in compliance with 44 CFR Part 201 on file with FEMA, applicants can use the **Find Plan** button to locate the electronic copy of the plan in the Plan Repository and auto-fill the plan information in this section. If the plan is not in the Plan Repository, applicants should enter the name, type, and approval date of the plan. If any other local mitigation plan has been adopted, the applicant should provide information by selecting the **Add Plan** button.
For project subgrant applications, applicants must describe how the proposed activity relates to or is consistent with the local and State/Tribal plans.

NOTE: The subgrant applicant is not required to enter information regarding the State/Tribal plan; however, if they do not, then the grant applicant must complete this portion when reviewing the subgrant application in order to approve the subgrant application (see Lesson 9).

Help Steve enter the Mitigation Plan Information section for the paper subgrant application. He will use the **Find Plan** button, since the City of Adversity has indicated that it has a FEMA-approved plan.

From the Application Status page , select the **Mitigation Plan Information link.** There are several required questions (indicated by a red asterisk) that need to be answered in this section.

Start by selecting the **Yes radio button**, indicating that there is a current mitigation plan, then select the **Find Plan button**. The Find Plan search screen is displayed.

You can search by: Plan Name, Plan Type, Plan Applicant, Jurisdiction Name, Jurisdiction (CID Number), Author, and/or Plan Status. In this case, you will search by plan type by selecting "Local Multihazard Mitigation Plan" from the **Plan Type drop-down list**. You can also choose to sort by Plan Name, Subgrant Name, or Grant Name. In this case, you will sort by the Plan Name by selecting "Plan Name" in the **Sort by drop-down list.** Select the **Search button** to initiate the search.

Select the radio button corresponding to the plan you are attaching to your application. In this case, select the radio button for the "Adversity Multihazard Mitigation Plan." Select the **Select Plan button**.

The plan information is automatically populated with the plan you have selected.

Mitigation Activity Information Section

The Mitigation Activity Information section collects basic information from the applicant on the activities being proposed. The applicant is required to choose one or more of the activities from a list of pre-defined activities with numeric identifiers. This information will help determine the eligibility of the activity type for different FEMA mitigation programs. For example, a Seismic Retrofit project may be eligible for a Pre-Disaster Mitigation (PDM) grant but not for a Flood Mitigation Assistance (FMA) grant.

NOTE: To see a list of the eligible mitigation activities for each grant program, click on the Help link.

Help Steve enter the Mitigation Activity Information section for the paper subgrant application. From the Sidebar menu, select the **Mitigation Activity Information link.**

To choose the type of proposed mitigation activity, select the **Add button.** A list of possible activities is displayed. Select the checkboxes for the type of activity you are proposing. You can choose multiple activities on this page. For this example, we will choose "Activity Code 103.1: Feasibility, Engineering, and Design Studies." After making your choice, select the **Add Activity button** to add the activity to the Mitigation Activity Information section of the application.

You can then scroll down to complete the remainder of the Mitigation Activity Information section. Check to make sure that the title of the proposed activity is correct. If it is incorrect, you can manually modify the text in the title field. **NOTE:** If you change the title of the Application here, the title will also be changed wherever else it appears in the system.

There are three required fields on this section-the type of proposed mitigation activity, the title of the application/proposed activity, and whether the proposed activity involves construction. When you have finished entering information, select the **Save and Continue button** to store the information.

Hazard Information Section

The Hazard Information section collects information about existing conditions and the hazard(s) to be mitigated in the geographic area to be addressed by the proposed activity. Applicants should clearly identify the source of the hazard(s) and how the hazard(s) caused previous damage, or how they could produce future damage. For project subgrant applications, this section allows the applicant to enter the latitude and longitude coordinates for the project area. In addition, applicants must provide information regarding the project's location within a floodplain or floodway.

This section is divided into several parts. To advance to the next part of this section, provide the requested information and select the **Save and Continue** button.

NOTE: This section is not included in Management Cost subgrant applications.

Scope of Work Section

The Scope of Work section collects more detailed information on the proposed activity. This section allows the applicant to provide specific information about the proposed activity, including a detailed description of the goals and objectives of the activity, the method proposed to complete the activity, and a schedule of tasks required to complete the activity. This level of detail will provide the grant applicant, as well as FEMA, sufficient information to evaluate the activity for eligibility and effectiveness.

Help Steve enter the Scope of Work section for the paper subgrant application. From the Sidebar menu, select the **Scope of Work link.**

This Scope of Work section has two parts. The first part includes several required fields, such as a description of the goals and objectives of the activity and a description of the methodology for implementing the activity. Once you have completed part 1, select the **Save and Continue button** to move to part 2.

In the second part of this section, you will specify the tasks involved in the project. Select the **Add Task button** to enter the first task. In the **Description of Task text field**, you are required to enter a description for the task. For Luciana's example, we will enter "Structure Demolition."

Next, you are required to enter a Starting Point for the task. Imagine the project has a timeline that starts at 1. Enter the number for the day (or week/month/year) on which the task will begin.

Luciana will begin the task in week 8. Enter the number 8 into the **Starting Point text field**. In the **Unit of Time drop-down menu** there are four choices: "Days," "Weeks," "Months," and "Years." For this example, we will select "Weeks."

Next, you are required to specify the expected length of the task in the **Duration text field.** For this example, our task is expected to last 16 weeks. Enter the number 16 in the **Duration text**

field and select "Weeks" from the **Unit of Time drop-down menu**.

You can also enter the name of the individual or contractor who will perform the work. This is not a required field. For this example, we will enter J.T. Demolition Services, Inc.

Select the **Save and Continue button** and the task will be added to the Scope of Work section. You can continue to add more tasks by selecting the **Add Task button** and entering all of the required data.

After all the tasks are entered, an estimate of the total duration of the proposed activity is required. Remember, it must be equal to, or exceed, the sum of the lengths of the individual tasks.

Properties Section

The Properties section allows the applicant to designate the properties to be mitigated for each project activity selected in the Mitigation Activity section. Before you can add a property to the Properties section, you have to complete the Mitigation Activity Information section. Of the activities you select from the Mitigation Activity Information section, some may require property information and some may not.

NOTE: This section is not included in Planning or Management Cost subgrant applications.

Properties Section (continued)

Depending on which activity is selected in the Mitigation Activity Information section, property information may be required. If more than one mitigation activity is selected, then the Properties section is broken out by the activities identified in the Mitigation Activity section.

To add a property for a particular mitigation activity, select the **Add Property** button for that activity. There are three steps to adding a property. First, the applicant will be required to enter the property address and information about the owner in Part 1: Property Information. Parts 2 and 3 collects specific information related to the property, such as age of structure, longitude/latitude and hazard information.

NOTE: You can also upload or import a list of properties from an Excel spreadsheet that will automatically populate the fields in the Add Property function.

Properties Section (continued)

Some mitigation activities do not require property information. For those activities where properties are not required, the **Property Information Not Applicable** checkbox is pre-selected and the **Add Property** and **Import Properties** buttons are not selectable. If you want to add properties to be mitigated for these activities, un-check the **Property Information Not**

Applicable checkbox and select the **Save** button. The **Add Property** and **Import Properties** buttons are now selectable.

Decision-Making Section

The Decision-Making section allows the applicant to describe the process you used to decide that this project is the best solution/alternative. The questions posed in this section help FEMA to evaluate the application.

NOTE: This section is not included in Planning or Management Cost subgrant applications. For project subgrant applications, none of the fields in this section is required. Therefore, when you first start the application, this section's status will be "Complete."

Cost Estimate Section

The Cost Estimate section allows the applicant to provide a detailed line item budget for each proposed mitigation activity. If more than one mitigation activity is proposed, then the Cost Estimate is broken out by the activities identified in the Mitigation Activity section.

Applicants must click the **Add Item** button to add each new cost item. Information required for each cost item includes the Item Name (i.e., general description of the cost), Subgrant Budget Class (e.g. personnel, supplies, equipment), Unit Quantity (e.g., 1,2,3,...n), Unit Measure (e.g., Each, Lump Sum, Acres, Cubic Feet, etc.), and Unit Cost per Item. The total of all cost items for all mitigation activities will be the total Cost Estimate for the subgrant.

Match Sources Section

The Match Sources section collects information regarding the required cost share for the subgrant application. For example, the Flood Mitigation Assistance (FMA) program requires a 75% / 25% cost share, by which up to 75% of the total project cost may be met by Federal grant funds and a minimum of 25% must be met from non-Federal funds. This section allows the applicant to identify the total match amount and the match sources. The match amount may be adjusted by percentage or by dollar amount.

Help Steve complete the Match Sources section for the paper subgrant application. From the Sidebar menu, select the **Match Sources link.**

Funding sources and dollar amounts are shown on this page. The **Proposed Federal Share** and **Proposed Non-Federal Share** are required fields.

To change the dollar amount of the Proposed Non-Federal share, select the **Proposed Non-Federal Share text field** and enter the dollar amount. This is the amount of money that will be contributed by local government and community funds. In this example, we are changing the Proposed Non-Federal Share from $963,240 (as displayed) to "$2,000,000."

Select the **Recalculate Share button** to determine the percentage represented by the revised Non Federal Share contributions.

Match Sources Section (continued)

The Match Sources section also allows the applicant to identify the source(s) of the non-Federal cost share and whether the match will be cash or in-kind services.

The applicant may list the match sources by clicking the **Add Match Source** button. Information required for each match source includes the Funding Source (e.g., State, Local, Private Non-Profit, Tribal, etc.), Name of the Funding Source, Funding Type (e.g., cash, labor, administration), and Amount. This section also has a placeholder for the date of availability of match and a place to attach the funds commitment letter.

NOTE: Subgrant applicants are not required to complete the Match Sources; however, if they do not, then the grant applicant must complete it when reviewing the subgrant application in order to approve the subgrant application (see Lesson 9).

Let's help Steve complete the second half of the Match Sources section for the paper subgrant application. In the top part of the Match Sources section, you calculated the Proposed Federal and Non-Federal Shares. In the bottom part of the section, you will be required to identify the sources of matching funds and to indicate whether the match will be in cash or in services.

After entering the new proposed amounts and recalculating the percentage shares, select the **Add Match Source button** to add the source of the matching funds.

There are four required fields on the Add Match Sources page—**Funding Source**, **Name of Funding Source**, **Funding Type**, and **Amount**.

Choose the **Funding Source** from the drop-down menu. The available choices are "Local Agency Funding," "Other Agency Funding," "Private Non-Profit Funding," and "State Agency Funding." For this example, we will choose "State Agency Funding**."**

Enter the **Name of the Funding Source** in the text box provided. For this example, we will enter Florida State Grant.

Choose the **Funding Type** from the drop-down menu. The available choices are "Administration," "Cash," "Consulting Fees," "Engineering Fees," "Equipment/Op Rental," "Labor," "Other," "Program Income," and "Supplies." For this example, we will choose "Equipment/Op Rental."

Enter the Amount of the Matched Funding in the text field provided. For this example, we will enter "$2,000,000.00."

Enter the **Date of Availability** of the Funds and **the Funds Commitment Letter Date** in the two text fields provided. The format of the dates should be MM-DD-YYYY. For this example, we will enter "09-27-2007" for the **Date of Availability** and "05-12-2005" for the **Funds Commitment Letter Date.**

Select the **Save and Continue button** to add the Match Source to the Match Sources section. You can add additional match sources by selecting the **Add Match Source button** and repeating the above process.

Cost Effectiveness Section

The Cost Effectiveness section collects information about the cost effectiveness of the proposed mitigation activity. The information to be provided here is based on a FEMA-approved cost-benefit analysis.

NOTE: Although this section is included for every subgrant application, planning and management cost activities are exempt from this analysis. Therefore, the full section is provied only for project subgrant applications.

This is a two-part section. The first part collects problem information and the second part collects damage history.

NOTE: For project subgrant applications, none of the fields in this section is required. Therefore, when you first start the application, the status of this section will be "Complete."

Environmental/Historic Preservation Information Section

The Environmental/Historic Preservation (EHP) Information section is included for every subgrant application. However, because most planning and management cost activities qualify for a Categorical Exclusion (CATEX), the full section is required to be completed only for project subgrant applications.

The section is broken down into an introduction and 11 parts—Parts A through K—covering relevant environmental laws and executive orders. Responses to each of these sections allow the reviewers to identify any potential environmental impacts that may result from the proposed mitigation project and to identify possible remedies to eliminate or lessen adverse impacts. For every question with a "Yes" or "Unknown" response, you are required to enter comments.

Note: Subgrant applicants are not required to complete this section; however, if they do not, then the grant applicant must complete it when reviewing the subgrant application in order to approve the subgrant application (see Lesson 9).

Help Steve enter the EHP Information section for the paper subgrant application. From the Sidebar menu, select the **Environmental/Historic Preservation Information link.**

This section will help you to identify the environmental and/or historic preservation impact of your project. There are several laws and executive orders with which FEMA must comply. In addition to the Introduction, this section has 11 parts, Sections A–K, that must be completed for project applications. Once you have completed each part, select the **Save and Continue button** to move to the next part. Or, you can use the drop-down menu to help you to navigate to the different parts of this section:

"Introduction"
"A. National Historic Preservation Act—Historic Buildings and Structures"
"B. National Historic Preservation Act—Archeological Resources"
"C. Endangered Species Act and Fish and Wildlife Coordination Act"
"D. Clean Water Act, Rivers and Harbors Act, and Executive Order 11990"
"E. Executive Order 11988 (Floodplain Management)"
"F. Coastal Zone Management Act"
"G. Farmland Protection Policy Act"
"H. RCRA and CERCLA (Hazardous and Toxic Materials)"
"I. Executive Order 12898"
"J. Other Environmental/Historic Preservations Laws or Issues"
"K. Summary and Cost of Potential Impacts"

For this example, we will choose "B. National Historic Preservation Act—Archeological Resources." Select the **Go button** to move to the part you selected.

Maintenance Schedule and Costs Section

The Maintenance Schedule and Costs section allows the applicant to identify a schedule and costs associated with the long-term maintenance of proposed projects. The subgrant applicant or the owner of the property to be mitigated is responsible for maintenance after the completion of a project. Therefore, any maintenance costs should **NOT** be included in the cost estimate. However, maintenance costs must be included in the benefit-cost analysis for the project.

NOTE: This section is not included in Planning or Management Cost subgrant applications. For project subgrant applications, none of the fields in this section is required. Therefore, when you first start the application, this section's status will be shown as "Complete."

Evaluation Information Section

The Evaluation Information section collects detailed information regarding project and planning activities for the Pre-Disaster Mitigation (PDM) grant program's National Ranking and Evaluation process. Specific details collected vary by application type and include:

- Community participation in programs such as the Community Rating System and Firewise Communities
- Desired outcomes, methodologies, performance expectations, timelines, milestones, and staff/resource plans
- Partners' involvement, long-term financial and social benefits, and outreach activities

- Percentage of population benefiting, as well as the cost-effectiveness (benefit-cost analysis) information for projects

NOTE: This section is required only for Project and Planning subgrant applications to be submitted by the grant applicant as part of a PDM grant application. The section may be completed by checking the "Not Applicable" checkbox for subgrant applications that are being submitted for consideration for other grant programs.

NOTE: This section is not included in Management Cost subgrant applications. Subgrant applicants are not required to complete all of the questions in this section; however, if they do not, then the grant applicant must complete them when reviewing the subgrant application in order to approve the subgrant application (see Lesson 9).

Comments and Attachments Section

The Comments and Attachments section will appear for Project, Planning, and Management Cost applications. This section gives an overview of all of the comments and attachments that the applicant has provided for each application section. It gives the applicant another opportunity to provide information not covered by the application sections, including any documentation to support information provided in the application. You can also update or delete comments or attachments you have added to other sections of the application.

- Comments are text only.
- Attachments may be any file type (e.g., Word documents, Excel spreadsheets, PDF files, etc.).

Help Steve enter the Comments and Attachment section for the paper subgrant application. From the Sidebar menu, select the **Comments and Attachments link.**

This section allows you to add a comment, or attach files, to supplement any section you have already completed. To attach a document to the application, select the **Add button.**

To identify the section of the application to which you wish to attach the document, select the **Name of Section drop-down menu.** All the sections of the application are listed in this drop-down menu. Select the section you wish to work on. For this example, we will choose "Scope of Work (Part 2)." You can also provide comments regarding the attachment by selecting and typing into the text field provided.

Scroll to the bottom of the page, and select the **Attachments button** to add a document attachment. The actual process involved in attaching a document will be discussed in the next topic: Electronic Files.

Electronic Files

Within the Comments and Attachments section, applicants are given the opportunity to attach various files that provide additional information to application reviewers. These files may be either paper or electronic.

Help Steve attach an electronic file in the Comments and Attachment section for the paper subgrant application. The City of Adversity has e-mailed a document to be included as part of its paper project application. Steve has saved it on his computer.

To attach an electronic file, select the **Attachments button** at the bottom of the Comments and Attachments section.

The Attach Document page appears. To upload an electronic file from your computer, select the **Electronic File radio button;** then scroll down to the Electronic File section of the page.

There are three required text fields in this section. They are **File Format, Compression Format,** and **Upload File.**

To identify the Operating System used on your computer, select it from the **Operating System drop-down menu**. The available choices are "Windows," "Macintosh," "UNIX," and "Other." For this example, we will choose "Windows."

To identify the software used to create the file you'll be attaching, select it from the **File Format drop-down menu**. The available choices are "MS Word," "MS Excel," "PDF," "WordPerfect," "Postscript," "ASCII Text," "Bitmap (bmp)," "Graphics Interchange format (gif)," "WordPerfect Graphics (wpg)," "JPEG Graphics (.jpg/.jpeg)," and "Other." **NOTE:** If the file format is already showing in the drop-down menu, you won't need to change this field. For this example, the format "MS Word" is already displayed so we do not need to change it.

Select the **Compression Format drop-down menu** to indicate whether the file is compressed (condensed to occupy less disk space)—and, if so, in which format it is compressed. The available choices are "None," "ZIP," "RAR," and "Other." For this example, we will choose "None."

To locate the file you wish to upload, select the **Browse button** next to the **Upload File text field**. Find the file on your computer and select it. For Windows users, after selecting the file, select the **Open button.** The file that you selected should appear in the **Upload File text field**.

Select the **Save and Continue button** and the selected file will appear as an attachment.

Paper Attachments

In many cases, documents to be attached within the Comments and Attachments section of a subgrant application may exist only in hard copy or paper form. In that case, the documents must be mailed. However, information about the mailed documents should be entered into the eGrants system to ensure a complete application file with reference to any non-electronic information.

The City of Adversity submitted a property inventory list that Steve is mailing to FEMA. For the text alternative, select the link below.

To attach a paper or hardcopy document, select the **Attachments button** at the bottom of the Comments and Attachments section.

The Attach Document page appears. To indicate that you are sending a document via the U.S. Postal Service, select the **Regular Mail radio button.**

So that the recipients will know when to expect the document, you'll need to tell them when it was sent. Select the **Mail Date text field** and enter the date in MM-DD-YYYY format. For this example, we will enter "11-20-2006."

Select the **Mail description text field** and enter a brief description of the item being sent. For this example, we will enter "Property inventory list" in the text field.

Select the **Save and Continue button** to confirm and return to the Comments and Attachments page. You will receive a summary of the documents you are mailing.

NOTE: Paper attachments are often hard to maintain and track. If you have the equipment to do so, scan paper attachments and send as an electronic attachment.

Assurances and Certifications Section

This section of the subgrant application will appear only if Assurances and Certifications is enabled by the grant applicant in the administration preferences (as described in Lesson 4). The Assurances and Certifications section is intended to provide documents listing Federal requirements for FEMA grants. There are four documents that may appear in this section. The first form listed in this section as Part I differs based on whether construction is proposed in the application.

FEMA Form 20-16A, Assurances Non-Construction Programs: This document asks applicants to certify that they will comply with a series of requirements including nondiscrimination, environmental standards, and audits. If the application circumstances do not include a Non-Construction program, select "Not Applicable" for this form.

FEMA Form 20-16B, Assurances Construction Programs: This document asks applicants to certify that they will comply with a series of requirements including nondiscrimination, environmental standards, and audits. If the application circumstances do not include a Construction program, select "Not Applicable" for this form.

FEMA Form 20-16C, Certification Regarding Lobbying; Debarment, Suspension and Other Responsibility Matters; and Drug-Free Workplace Requirements: This document asks applicants to certify regarding lobbying, debarment, suspension, and other responsibility matters as well as drug-free workplace requirements.

SF-LLL, Disclosure of Lobbying Activities: This document asks applicants to disclose their lobbying activities. Complete this only if you are applying for a grant of more than $100,000 and have lobbying activities using non-Federal funds. If those circumstances do not apply, select "Not Applicable" for this form.

Lesson Summary

- The Subapplicant Information section requires detailed information about the organization requesting the subgrant.
- The Contact section collects information about whom to contact if there are questions about the application.
- The Community section requires information about the specific community requesting assistance.
- The Mitigation Plan section collects information about the local and State/Tribal FEMA-approved mitigation plan.
- The Scope of Work section identifies and collects information for specific mitigation activities.
- The Properties section collects information about the properties to be mitigated by each project activity selected in the Scope of Work section.

Lesson Summary (continued)

In this lesson, you learned about the specifics of various sections of the eGrants system.

Some key points from this lesson:

- The Cost Estimate section requires the detailed line item budget for each proposed activity selected in the Mitigation Activity section.
- The Cost Share section collects information about the non-Federal cost share for the grant, including the total match amount/percentage and the match source.
- The Cost Effectiveness section allows you to provide information about the cost effectiveness of the proposed project.
- The Environmental/Historic Preservation Review section collects information regarding the historic and environmental impact of the proposed project.
- The Evaluation section collects detailed information regarding projects and planning for the PDM grant program's National Ranking and Evaluation process.
- The Comments and Attachments section allows the applicant to add and update supporting documents and information to the application.
- The Assurances and Certifications section requires that the applicant complete required documents for various Federal and FEMA regulations.

Lesson 7: Access to Applications

Lesson Overview

Upon completion of this lesson, you should be able to:

- Provide another individual access to an application
- Update another individual's access to an application
- Revoke deny another individual's access to an application

Scenario

State Official: Steve Miller

Agency: State of Florida

Problem: Steve works for the Florida Emergency Management Agency and recently applied for a eGrants account. He was only given View/Print and Create/Edit access.

To Date: Steve has entered in most of the paper subgrant application and knows that the next step will include completing and submitting the paper subgrant application.

Next Step: Steve does not have Sign/Submit access; he will need to provide his supervisor, Deborah Johnson, Director of the State of Florida Emergency Management Agency, access to the paper application so that she can submit it.

Audio Transcript: Hello. I'm Steve and I have entered a paper subgrant application for the City of Adversity. I'm almost finished, but my supervisor, Deborah, will need to Sign/Submit the application. I need to provide her access to the application.

Why Provide Access?

In eGrants, users have the ability to grant, update, or revoke access to their applications. Reasons to grant someone else access to an application include the following:

1. **Vacation:** Bill is creating a subgrant application, but is about to leave for a two-week vacation. He doesn't want work on the application to stop while he's gone. He gives Teresa, a co-worker, access to the application so she can continue entering data in his absence.
2. **Advice:** Sayid, a new employee, has completed his first application, but isn't sure that everything was entered correctly. He gives Claire, a more experienced eGrants user, access to his subgrant application so that she can check his work and make sure that it is correct.

3. **Sharing:** Debbie, Anne, and Jennifer are all involved in a proposed project to reduce recurring damage caused by coastal erosion. They are completing a subgrant application in hopes of receiving funds for their project. Debbie creates the application and provides access to Anne and Jennifer so that they may help enter the project data.
4. **Copying:** James has asked Rob to provide him access to the application that Rob created last year so that James may copy it when creating a new application for a similar activity.
5. **Authority:** In Steve's case, he does not have Sign/Submit access in eGrants, and therefore cannot Sign/Submit any applications he enters into eGrants. He will need to provide his supervisor, Deborah, access to his applications so that she can sign and submit them, as well as any award packages and quarterly reports that would be associated with them if approved by FEMA.

NOTE: In some cases, FEMA may reassign permission to all of a grant user's applications to another grant user, allowing the other user access to the applications. Currently, this is irreversible; therefore, it should be requested only on an as-needed basis (e.g., if someone retires without granting access to their applications to another user). This functionality is similar to the grant user's ability to reassign permission to subgrant users' applications.

Levels of Access

When allowing someone access to an application, different levels of access can be selected. More than one level may be selected.

1. **Sign/Submit:** This is the highest level of access, and it allows applicants to review, sign, and submit applications.
2. **Create/Edit:** This is the middle level of access, and it allows users to view, create, and update applications.
3. **View/Print:** This is the lowest level of access, and it allows users only to see application data and print the information.

The levels of access that you can set are also dependent upon the user's access to applications.

For example, you can not provide a co-worker Sign/Submit access if they only have Create/Edit access in applications.

Business Rules

There are a few business rules related to the provision of access. The first rule states that any application owner may authorize or revoke access to that application to other grant users in their State, Territory, or Tribal area. However, the additional user's authorized role will determine the highest level of access he or she may be granted to any application. In addition, local officials can share their applications with state officials prior to submitting their subgrant applications.

Example: Sean, a state official in Pennsylvania, has Sign/Submit-level access in eGrants. He wants to provide his co-worker Grace access to his application. However, Grace has a

Create/Edit level of access. Therefore, Sean may not provide Grace Sign/Submit access to his application, but he may provide her Create/Edit access.

Example: Katie, a state official in New Jersey, has Create/Edit level access in eGrants. She wants to provide her supervisor Frank access to her application. She has completed the application and is ready for it to be reviewed and submitted. Frank has a Sign/Submit level of access to eGrants.

Therefore, Katie may provide Frank Sign/Submit access to her application.

Authorizing Access

Access may be authorized for any submitted or unsubmitted subgrant or grant application(s). Steve wishes to grant Deborah, his supervisor, access to the paper City of Adversity Floodprone Property Acquisition application so that she can sign and submit it.

To find the access options from the Grant Applicant Home Page, select the appropriate link to **work on the un-submitted or submitted subgrant or grant Application**. Help Steve search for Deborah to give her that access.

From the Grant Applicant Home Page, select the **Work on Un-submitted Paper Subgrant Applications link.** A list of all un-submitted paper subgrant applications (for which you have access) are displayed.

Under the **Authorize/Revoke Access column** for the application, you are providing access to, select the **View Details link**. In this case, you are providing access to the City of Adversity Floodprone Property Acquisition application.

Select the **Authorize Access button**. You can now search for the user(s) you want to authorize. Choose one or more criteria to search for the person who will receive access: first name, last name, e-mail address, or agency. You can also sort by the search criteria and choose how many results to display per page. In this case, we will search by the person's last name—Johnson. As only one of the four fields must be completed, you may skip the others. Now, choose the way in which you would like to see the results sorted. In this case, select "Last Name" in the **Sort by drop-down list**. To determine the number of results displayed on a given page, select the **Results Per Page drop-down list**. Select "10" results to appear on each page.

Select the **Search button** to initiate the search.

Names matching your search are displayed.

Access Level and Time

In addition to assigning someone a specific level of access, users must limit the duration of that access. However, the duration is fairly open-ended.

Steve wishes to provide Deborah Sign/Submit access to the City of Adversity Floodprone Property Acquisition paper application. Steve does not need to limit Deborah's access time, but he wants to learn how to do that. Therefore, he will limit her access to two weeks.

In order to set the access time limit for Deborah, start with the information from the search described in the previous screen. Select the radio button that represents the person to whom you wise to give access to. In this case select the radio button next to Deborah Johnson's name. Select the **Authorize Access button.**

You will then have to decide what type of access you wish to provide the user. You can provide them with View/Print, Create/Edit, or Sign/Submit access. In this case you wish to provide Deborah with all three types of access, so you will select the **View/Print check box,** the **Create/Edit check box,** and the **Sign/Submit check box.** To identify the duration of access, type the length in the **Period of Time field**. In this case, we will enter in the "2."

Then select select the appropriate unit of time from the **Unit of Time drop-down list**. You can select Days(s), Weeks(s), Month(s), or Year(s). In this case we will select "Week(s)."

In the **Justifications field,** explain why the access is necessary. In this case you would enter "Need someone with Sign/Submit access to sign and submit the paper subgrant application." Select the **Save and Continue button.**

When access is authorized, the Authorize/Revoke Access screen appears. From here, you can change the access or return to the Grant Applicant Home Page.

Updating Access

For a variety of reasons, users may need to update or change the level or duration of access they've provided to other users.

It has been almost two weeks since Steve provided Sign/Submit access to Deborah for the City of Adversity Property Acquisition paper application. She hasn't had time to go in and sign and submit the application. Steve will need to extend Deborah's access time.

Start from the Authorize/Access screen. Find the application for which the access rights will be modified and select the corresponding **View Details link.** In this case, we are updating access to the City of Adversity Floodprone Property Acquisition application. Select the **Update link** corresponding to the person whose access you are modifying. In this case, Deborah Johnson.

To update the period of time, enter the updated number into the **Period of Time field.** In this case, enter 3 and select "Month(s)" from the **Unit of Time drop-down list.** Select the **Save and Continue Button.**

Revoking Access

From time to time, a situation might arise in which a user needs to revoke someone's access to an application (e.g. if a user retires or leaves the organization).

Steve does not need to revoke Deborah's access, but if he needed to, the process is similar to the process for Updating the access. Instead of selecting the **Update** link, you select the **Deny/Revoke** link, confirm that you really do want to deny/revoke access, and the person's access will be revoked.

Lesson Summary

- eGrants users may provide individuals access to applications, update that access, or revoke the access.
- From lowest to highest, access levels are View/Print, Create/Edit, and Sign/Submit.
- The business rule for both grant and subgrant users is that they may not provide individuals with greater access to any application than that individual's authorized level permits.

Lesson 8: Un-submitted Paper Subgrant Applications

Lesson Overview

Upon completion of this lesson, you should be able to:

- View un-submitted paper subgrant applications
- Update un-submitted paper subgrant applications
- Submit paper subgrant applications

Scenario

State Official: Steve

Community: State of Florida

Problem: The State has received a paper subgrant application from the City of Adversity. The project application proposes to acquire and demolish 54 buildings along the Quake River that have experienced repetitive flooding.

To Date: Steve has entered most of the paper subgrant application.

Next Step: Steve will need to complete the remaining sections of the paper subgrant application in order to submit it.

(Audio Transcript)

Hello. I'm Steve and I work for the state of Florida. Last week, I entered into eGrants a paper subgrant application received from the City of Adversity. So far, I've filled out 16 sections of the application. Now, I'm going to complete the remaining two sections of this application in order to submit it.

Un-submitted Applications

Often, users will not have all the information necessary to complete an application when they first create it. Applications may be in different stages of development. Some sections may be complete, while others may require additional information. eGrants allows users to create the application, enter some information, save the application, and then return at a later time to update and complete it.

To facilitate this process, eGrants allows users to search for existing applications to update. These are found under the Un-Submitted Applications menu option because they have not been submitted.

To search for and update/edit existing paper subgrant applications, select the **Work on Un-submitted Paper Subgrant Application(s)** link from the Grant Applicant Home Page.

Update an Application

After searching for and finding the desired application, users will see the Application Status screen which lists various sections in that application. Next to each section, its status will be listed. The status will be either incomplete or complete. Before an application is submitted, all sections must be complete (i.e., have a status of "complete"). To work on a section, you may select either the Incomplete or Complete link or the section name in the sidebar menu.

After working on an application section, it is important to save the data by selecting the Save or Save and Continue button at the bottom of the screen.

Completing a Section

After working on an application section, the user will face a decision:

- If the application is ready for submission, the user may select **Review and Submit Application** from the **Sidebar** menu. Only users with Sign/Submit access for applications in eGrants may submit an application.
- If the application is not ready for submission, the user may select **Return to Home Page** from the **Sidebar** menu.

Submission

When all sections of the paper subgrant application have a status of "complete," the application may be submitted. Only users with Sign/Submit access for applications may submit an application in eGrants. The **Review and Submit** option in the **Sidebar** menu facilitates this process.

Steve has confirmed that the paper application is ready for submission. Only eGrants users with Sign/Submit authority may submit an application. Remember, Steve does **not**have Sign/Submit access, so his supervisor, Deborah, must sign the application.

(Show Me Simulation Transcript)

From the Application Status screen, select the **Review and Submit Application** link in the Sidebar menu.

To sign the application, enter your password into the **Password** field. In this case, Deborah's password is "florida1".

Select the electronic signature verification check box.

Select the **Submit Application** button.

You should receive verification that your application has been submitted.

(Audio Transcript)

Hi, I'm Deborah. I am the Director of the Florida Emergency Management Agency. Steve has informed me that he has entered a paper application into the eGrants system. Since he does not have Sign/Submit access, I will sign and submit the application. Let's get started!

Lesson Summary

In this lesson, you learned about how to

- View un-submitted paper subgrant applications
- Update un-submitted paper subgrant applications
- Submit paper subgrant applications

Some key points from this lesson:

- Users may begin an application in one eGrants session and complete it in a different session.
- When returning to eGrants to update a paper application already begun, users should choose the **Work on Un-submitted Paper Subgrant Application(s)** link from the Grant Applicant Home Page.
- eGrants users must have Sign/Submit access in eGrants to submit a completed paper subgrant application.

Lesson 9: Reviewing Subgrant Applications

Lesson Overview

Upon completion of this lesson, you should be able to:

- Check out subgrant applications
- Review subgrant applications
- Request revisions on subgrant applications
- Approve, disapprove, or release subgrant applications to stockpile
- Check in subgrant applications

Scenario

State Official: Steve

Community: State of Florida

Problem: In order for Steve to be able to include subgrant applications from subgrant applicants in a grant application to FEMA he will need to review and approve the subgrant applications.

Next Step: Steve will now review a submitted subgrant application and then approve it, disapprove it, request a revision, or release it to the stockpile.

(Audio Transcript)

Hello. I'm Steve and I work for Florida EMA. I will need to spend some time reviewing subgrant applications submitted from communities in my state in preparation for starting a grant application to FEMA. Before any of the subgrant applications can be included in a grant application, they will need to be reviewed and approved.

Reviewing Subgrant Applications

Grant users must review and approve subgrant applications from their subgrant applicants before the subgrant applications can be attached to a grant application.

Subgrant applications can be viewed only by the subgrant applicant's State, Indian Tribe, or Territory. Other States, Indian Tribes, or Territories may not view the subgrant application.

In order to review the subgrant application, you will need to check out the application, review it, and then check in the application. You can also review Un-submitted subgrants if a subgrant applicant gives you access to assist them.

NOTE: Grant applicants do not have to review their own grant as subgrant applications.

Checking Out Applications

In any given State or Tribal Government acting as a grant applicant, there may be one or more registered users with review and/or approval rights for applications. To ensure that only one person is working on a particular subgrant application at any given time, you must first check out the application.

Checking out a subgrant application allows you to review (access, add comments, request revisions, approve) the application. While a subgrant application is checked out to you, no other users can work on the application. Other users may view (read only) the subgrant application, but may not check out or review the application.

Steve wishes to review the paper subgrant application that he entered into eGrants several weeks ago. The following simulation will illustrate how to check out the subgrant application. Select the Play button to begin the simulation.

NOTE: In order to check out applications, you must have ***at minimum*** Create/Edit access for applications.

NOTE: The Check Out Subgrant Applications screen defaults to display subgrant applications with Submitted to Stockpile status, meaning that they have not yet been checked out and reviewed. To display other subgrant applications, select a status from the drop down list and click the Go button or click the Search button to search for a particular subgrant application by number, title, subgrant applicant, subgrant type, activity type, etc.

(Show Me Simulation Transcript)

From the Grant Applicant Home Page, select the **Review Submitted Subgrant Application(s)** link.

Select **Check Out Subgrant Applications** link, located on the sidebar menu.

Find the application you want to check out and select the check box. For this scenario, select the check box for the City of Adversity Floodprone Property Acquisition application.

Select the **Check Out Applications** button.

When asked if you are sure you want to check out the applications listed, select the **Yes** button.

The application you selected to check out should now be listed on the Review Subgrant Applications screen.

Reviewing a Subgrant Application

To begin reviewing a subgrant application you have checked out, select the **Review Submitted Subgrant Application(s)** link. Next select the **Review** link corresponding to the application you wish to review. This will display the status screen for the application. From here, you can review each section by selecting the **Complete/Incomplete** link in the status column.

As a grant applicant, for each subgrant application you review, you can:

- **Approve** the subgrant application
- **Request Revisions** to request additional information from the subgrant applicant and to increase the subgrant application's chances of approval and inclusion in a grant application
- **Release to Stockpile**, or
- **Disapprove** the subgrant application

Additionally, there are several sections that have fields that require the grant applicant's input. These sections are indicated by a "Yes" in the status screen under the **Section to be Completed** column.

NOTE: The Stockpile is simply a collection of the applications that have been neither approved nor disapproved—like putting the subgrant applications in a file drawer.

Sections to be Completed

Depending on the type of application you are reviewing, there are different sections that require input from the grant applicant. The table below shows which sections need to be completed by the grant applicant for the various application types.

Revisions

As you are reviewing the subgrant applications, you may determine that additional information is needed, or that a change or correction needs to be made by the subgrant applicant. In addition, a subgrant applicant may request that a subgrant application be released for updating after it has been submitted. In these cases, you can send a Revision Request to the subgrant applicant. The subgrant application will be returned to the subgrant applicant for revision.

If you have enabled external e-mail as an Administrative Preference, you can then review and revise or add to the e-mail that will be sent to the subgrant applicant POC notifying him or her of the revision request.

The City of Adversity application that Steve is reviewing does not require a revision request, but Steve wants to learn how to complete the revision requests.

(Show Me Simulation Transcript)

From the Review Subgrant Application screen, scroll down to the bottom of the screen and select the **Request Revision** radio button.

Set a revision deadline. For this scenario, enter "07-03-2012" into the **Set Revision Deadline** field.

Select the **Add Comment** button.

Enter comments in the Comments to Subgrantee section of the Add/Modify Comments screen explaining the revision you would like made. In this case, enter "Please include a more detailed Scope of Work" in the **Comments to Subgrantee** field.

Select the **Save and Continue** button on the Add/Modify Comments screen.

Select the **Save and Continue** button on the Review Subgrant Application screen.

If you have enabled external e-mail in the administrative preferences, you may verify the e-mail message and select the **Send Email** button to send an e-mail notifying the subgrant applicant POC that a revision had been requested on his or her subgrant application. After e-mail confirmation, or if external e-mail is not enabled, you can select the **Return to Review Applications** button to review other subgrant applications.

Approve, Disapprove, Release to Stockpile

In addition to requesting a revision, you can also choose to approve, disapprove, or release the subgrant to stockpile. Remember, the **Approve** radio button does not become active until all of the sections have been reviewed and their status is "Complete."

Select the appropriate review status radio button and then select the **Save and Continue** button.

If you have enabled external e-mail as an Administrative Preference, you can then review and revise or add to the e-mail that will be sent to the subgrant applicant POC notifying him or her of the status of the subgrant application.

Checking in Applications

When you have completed your review, remember that you have to check in the subgrant application. When an application is checked out to you, no one else can access it, and it cannot be included in a grant application.

NOTE: This means that if you have requested a revision, but have not checked the application in, the subgrant applicant cannot make the revisions you requested.

Steve has completed his review of the City of Adversity subgrant application and wishes to check in the application. The following simulation will illustrate how to check in the subgrant application. Select the Play button to begin the simulation.

(Show Me Simulation Transcript)

From the Grant Applicant Home Page, select the **Review Submitted Subgrant Application(s)** link.

The Overview screen shows you any applications you already have checked out and the number of applications available to be checked out. Select the **Check In Subgrant Applications** link in the Sidebar menu.

Find the application you want to check in and check the box in the **Select** column. In this case, you are checking in the City of Adversity Floodprone Property Acquisition application.

Select the **Check In Applications** button.

When asked if you are sure you want to check in the application listed, select the **Yes** button. The application you selected to check in should now be removed from the list of checked out applications.

Lesson Summary

- In this lesson, you learned about how to
    - Check out subgrant applications
    - Review subgrant applications
    - Request revisions on subgrant applications
    - Approve, disapprove, or release subgrant applications to stockpile
    - Check in subgrant applications

  Some key points from this lesson:

    - In order to begin reviewing a subgrant application, the grant applicant must check out the application.
    - While the subgrant application is checked out, other users can view the application, but cannot work on it. This means that if you have requested a revision, but have not checked the application in, the subgrant applicant cannot make the revisions you requested.
    - Grant applicants can choose to approve, disapprove, release to stockpile, or request revisions to a subgrant application.
    - There are sections that need to be completed by the grant applicant. These sections are marked in the Sections to be Completed column on the review status page. The specific sections that need to be completed depend on the type of application that is being reviewed.

Lesson 10: Creating a Grant as Subgrant Application

Lesson Overview

Upon completion of this lesson, you should be able to:

- Identify the sections of a grant as subgrant application with fields that differ from a subgrant application
- Create/copy a grant as subgrant application
- Complete the Cost Estimate section for a grant as subgrant application

Scenario

State Official: Steve Miller

Community: State of Florida

Problem: Steve needs to create a Management Costs subgrant application for the State.

To Date: Steve has entered subgrant applications received on paper and reviewed subgrant applications in eGrants.

Next Step: Steve will create a grant as subgrant application to apply for management costs for the State.

(Audio Transcript)

Hello. I'm Steve and I work for the State of Florida. My supervisor asked me to prepare a grant as subgrant application for management costs required to manage the subgrants that will be included in our grant application to FEMA. Although I have created paper subgrant applications and reviewed subgrant applications, I need to learn how grant as subgrant applications differ from subgrant applications. Let's get started.

Grant as Subgrant Applications

States or Indian Tribal governments can apply for mitigation funds for projects, planning activities, or applicant management costs by completing a grant as subgrant application.

The grant as subgrant application sections are the same as in subgrant applications completed by subgrant applicants for each application type. However, there are a few fields in some of the sections of the grant as subgrant application that are different.

These are the fields that the grant applicant completed in the review phase for subgrant applications. The grant applicant will not review grant as subgrant applications.

Grant as Subgrant Application Variations

There are several sections with fields that differ between a grant as subgrant application and a subgrant application. Select each section below to learn about the differences.

Section	Differences
Applicant Information	For PDM-C grants, the grant applicant must answer the question asking if the applicant is a small, impoverished community.
Cost Estimate	The **Grant Budget Class** column and the **Subgrant Budget Class** column are required to be completed in grant as subgrant applications.
Match Sources	The grant applicant must complete both the **Non-Federal Cost Share** field and **Match Sources** (except for RFC grants).
Evaluation Information	For planning and project grant as subgrant applications, all of the questions in this four-part section are required for grant applicants.
Assurances and Certifications	For subgrant applications, inclusion of this section is determined by the grant applicant in the Administrative Preferences. If the Assurances and Certifications section is turned on, it is required for grant applicants to complete in grant as subgrant applications.

NOTE: The Evaluation Information section is not included in the Management Costs Application. It may be indicated as "not applicable" for planning and project subgrant applications unless intended for a PDM grant.

Community Information Section

The **Community Information** section in a grant as subgrant application is the same as in a subgrant application. However, for grant as subgrant applications, if the benefit of the proposed activity is statewide (such as developing a state plan or applicant management costs), then the grant user should select "Statewide" from the community listing.

Management Cost Subgrant Applications

Management Cost subgrant applications can be completed for activities that are directly related to the administration of programs, grants, and/or promotion of mitigation activities. Of the three application types, Management Cost Applications have the fewest number of sections.

Creating or Copying a Grant as Subgrant Application

Just like subgrant applications, grant as subgrant applications can be created either by starting a new application or by copying an existing grant as subgrant application.

Cost Estimate Section

The Cost Estimate section in a grant as subgrant application provides a detailed line item budget for the proposed activity, including both grant and subgrant budget classes for each line item.

Steve has started his grant as subgrant Management Cost application. As a grant applicant, Steve will need to provide both the grant and subgrant budget classes for each line item.

(Show Me Simulation Transcript)

From the Application Status screen, select the **Cost Estimate** link in the Sidebar menu.

To add a cost line item, select the **Add Item** button.

Select the **Item Name** field to enter the item name. In this case, "Paper".

Select the **Grant Budget Class** drop-down menu. This drop-down menu has nine options. For this scenario, select the "Supplies" items.

Select the **Subgrant Budget Class** drop-down menu. This drop-down menu has nine options. For this scenario, select the "Supplies" item.

Select the **Unit Quantity** field to enter the unit quantity. In this case, the unit quantity is "100".

Select the **Unit of Measure** drop-down menu. This drop-down menu has 18 options. Select the "Each" item.

Select the **Unit Cost** field to enter the unit cost. In this case, the unit cost is "25.00".

Select the **Save and Continue** button.

The item you added should now appear in the list in the Cost Estimate section. You can now add addition items.

Lesson Summary

In this lesson, you learned about:

- The sections of a grant as subgrant application with fields that differ from a subgrant application
- Grant as subgrant application
- The Cost Estimate section for a grant as subgrant application

Some key points from this lesson:

- States, Indian Tribal governments, and territories can apply for FEMA funds for projects, planning activities, or applicant management costs by completing a grant as subgrant application.
- The grant as subgrant application has several sections with fields that differ from the subgrant application: Applicant Information, Cost Estimate, Match Sources, and Evaluation Information.
- The grant applicant will not review grant as subgrant applications.
- Both the grant and subgrant budget classes must be provided in the Cost Estimate section of grant as subgrant applications.
- For proposed activity with statewide benefit (such as developing a state plan or applicant management costs), the grant user should select "Statewide" from the community listing in the Community Information section.
- The Assurance and Certifications section must be completed for grant as subgrant applications if it is turned on in the administrative preferences.

Lesson 11: Un-submitted Grant as Subgrant Applications

Lesson Overview

Upon completion of this lesson, you should be able to:

- View un-submitted grant as subgrant applications
- Update un-submitted grant as subgrant applications
- Delete un-submitted grant as subgrant applications
- Submit a grant as subgrant application

Scenario

State Official: Steve Miller

Community: State of Florida

Problem: Steve has been working on a grant as subgrant Management Cost application.

Next Step: Steve will now need to complete his un-submitted application.

(Audio Transcript)

Hello. I'm Steve and I work for the State of Florida. I have been working on completing a grant as subgrant Management Cost Application. I didn't have all of the data ready when I started, but now I am ready to complete the application. Once I have completed the application, I will ask my supervisor, Deborah, to sign and submit the application so that it will be available to include in a grant application. I have already given Deborah access to the application.

View Un-submitted Applications

Applications are often in different stages of development. eGrants allows users to start their grant as subgrant applications and come back at a later time to complete them.

You can view any un-submitted application by selecting the **Work on Un-submitted Subgrant Application** link from the Grant Applicant Homepage

Update Un-submitted Applications

The Subgrant Status page lists each of the applications that you have started, but not submitted. You can make changes to any application by selecting the **Update** link.

When Steve began the application, he did not have the Federal Employer Identification (EIN) Number for the **Applicant Information** section. He has now been provided this and will need to enter it into the application to complete this section.

Delete Un-submitted Grant as Subgrant Application

eGrants also allows users to delete un-submitted grant as subgrant applications.

Reasons that users might choose to delete an un-submitted application include the following:

- The information in the application is no longer current and it would be easier to start over than to make individual changes to the current application.
- There are old applications that have never been submitted.
- An application has been created by mistake.

Make sure you really should delete the application; once it's deleted, you will not be able to recover the data in that application.

(Show Me Simulation Transcript)

From the Grant Applicant Home Page, select the **Work on Un-Submitted Subgrant Application(s)** link.

Select the checkbox corresponding to the application you wish to delete. In this case you will delete the Floodprone Property Acquisition application.

Select the **Delete Application** button.

Select the **Yes** button when asked if you are sure you want to delete the application. The application you have selected has been deleted.

Submit an Un-submitted Grant as Subgrant Application

Once all of the sections are labeled "Complete," Steve will need to ask his supervisor to sign and submit the 2008 Florida EMA Management Cost Application. He has given access to the grant as subgrant application to her just as he did for the paper subgrant application he created for the City of Adversity.

The process for submittal of grant as subgrant applications is very similar to the Sign/Submit process for paper subgrant applications. To sign and submit the grant as subgrant application, the grant user who has Sign/Submit access for applications electronically signs the application by:

- Entering his or her Password
- Selecting the checkbox stating that he/she is signing the application

Lesson Summary

- In this lesson, you learned about how to:
    - View un-submitted grant as subgrant applications
    - Update un-submitted grant as subgrant applications
    - Delete un-submitted grant as subgrant applications
    - Submit a grant as subgrant application

Some key points from this lesson:

- You can view, update, delete, and submit grant as subgrant applications just as you can with paper subgrant applications.
- eGrants allows users to begin working on applications and come back at later time(s) to complete them.
- You can update both complete and incomplete sections of an un-submitted application.
- eGrants allows users to delete applications, but once deleted, the data in the applications is not retrievable.
- In order to sign and submit the application, the grant user with Sign/Submit access for applications needs to enter his/her Password for the eGrants system and select the checkbox stating that he/she is signing the application.

Lesson 12: Creating a Grant Application

Lesson Overview

Upon completion of this lesson, you should be able to:

- Create/copy a grant application
- Complete the Applicant Information section
- Complete the Contact Information section
- Complete the Subgrant Applications section
- Complete the Schedule section
- Complete the Budget section
- Complete the Properties section
- Complete the Comments and Attachments section
- Complete the Assurance and Certifications section

Scenario

State Official: Steve Miller

Community: State of Florida

Problem: Steve has been tasked with creating a grant application that will be submitted to FEMA.

Next Step: Steve will need to create the application, complete the sections, and have his supervisor sign and submit it.

Audio Transcript: Hello. I'm Steve and I work for the State of Florida. I have worked on creating paper subgrant applications, reviewing and approving subgrant applications, and creating grant as subgrant applications. Now I am going to create a PDM grant application to include approved subgrant applications that will be submitted to FEMA. Let's get started!

(Audio Transcript)

Hello. I'm Steve and I work for the State of Florida. I have worked on creating paper subgrant applications, reviewing and approving subgrant applications, and creating grant as subgrant applications. Now I am going to create a PDM grant application to include approved subgrant applications that will be submitted to FEMA. Let's get started!

Grant Applications

FEMA's mitigation grant programs provide funding for eligible mitigation activities that reduce disaster losses and protect life and property from future disaster damages. FEMA provides these mitigation grants to eligible grant applicant State/Tribes/Territories that in turn provide subgrants to local governments.

Beginning a Grant Application

The process to start a grant application is very similar to that for starting the paper subgrant application and the grant as subgrant application. Grant applicants can choose to create a new grant application or to copy information from an existing grant application. The grant application sections are the same for each of the grant application types. Several sections of a grant application are similar to the subgrant application sections. Once an application has been started, you can select the Incomplete link for each section to complete that section.

Applicant Information

The **Applicant Information** section collects information on the name of the applicant, the type of the applicant, and other identifying information just like the subgrant and grant as subgrant applications.

NOTE: Remember to use the Search function to fill in the Organization field to help prevent the creation of different versions of the name of the organization.

Contact Information

The **Contact Information** section, as for subgrant and grant as subgrant applications, collects information on whom to contact if there are questions about the application. This section requires at least one Point of Contact (POC). An alternate POC is not required, but is suggested. The POC(s) will receive e-mail messages from FEMA regarding the status of the grant application.

Subgrant Applications

In the **Subgrant Applications** section, grant applicants select the approved subgrant applications that they would like to attach to the grant application, including the subgrant applications that they have reviewed and approved and any grant as subgrant applications that they created.

This section:

- Lists the currently attached subgrants
- Allows grant users to search for subgrant applications that have already been attached
- Allows grant users to add/update/delete subgrants to the grant application

In order to add subgrant applications, select the **Add Subgrant Application(s)** button. All of the subgrant applications and grant as subgrant applications that have been approved and checked in are listed. Remember, grant as subgrant applications are automatically approved.

Errors

When searching for subgrants to include in the **Subgrant Applications** section, you may find that some of the subgrant applications have error code(s) displayed in the Select column and are not selectable. Therefore, they cannot be attached to the grant application type that you are creating.

The descriptions of the error codes appear in the footer of the page below the list of applications. For example, e1 (error 1) is defined this way: "Some of the mitigation activities selected within the 'Mitigation Activity Information' section are not eligible for this grant program."

If an error can be fixed in order to make a subgrant eligible for the grant program for which you are creating a grant application, you can select the **Review & Approval** link or return to the Grant Applicant Home Page and go to the **Review Subgrant Application** section.

Adding Subgrant Applications

You can select any of the eligible, approved subgrants that you want to attach to your grant application. Once any corrections have been made for subgrants with errors, you may attach them as well.

(Show Me Simulation Transcript)

To begin attaching subgrant applications, from the Subgrant Applications screen select the **Add Subgrant Application(s)** button.

Check the checkbox in the **Select** column corresponding to the applications you want to include in the grant application. For this scenario, we will select 3 applications. Select the checkbox for the Tampa Bay Mitigation Projects application. Select the checkbox for the Florida EMA Management Cost application. Select the checkbox for the City of Adversity Floodprone Property Acquisition application.

Select the **Add Subgrant Application(s)** button.

Select the **Yes** button to confirm that you want to attach the selected subgrants.

The subgrants you have selected have been added. To complete ranking subgrant applications, see the next simulation.

Ranking Subgrant Applications

Once you have confirmed which applications to add to your grant application, you will also need to rank each application. The ranking of the subgrants differs, depending on the type of grant you are applying for.

For PDM grant applications, each subgrant application needs to be assigned a unique rank from 1 (highest priority) to X, where X is the total number of subgrants attached to the grant application.

For FMA, RFC, and SRL grant applications, you assign a rank of 1 (high), 2 (medium), or 3 (low) priority to each subgrant application

(Show Me Simulation Transcript)

To begin ranking the subgrant application, from the Edit Subgrant Ranks screen input numbers into the text box in the Rank column. In this case the City of Adversity Floodprone Acquisition application is ranked "1". The Tampa Bay Mitigation Projects application is ranked "2". The Florida EMA Management Cost application is ranked "3".

Select the **Save and Continue** button.

The subgrant applications have been attached and ranked.

Updating Attached Subgrants

You may find that you need to update subgrant applications that you have attached to your grant application.

To update a subgrant application that you have attached to your grant application, select the **Update** link in the **Action** column next to the subgrant application. Select the **Complete** link in the **Status** column next to the application section that you wish to update. When you have finished the application, select the **Save and Continue** button on the Update Subgrant Application page to return to the Subgrant Applications section of the grant application.

NOTE: You will only be able to update the information in the fields populated by the grant applicant. If information provided by the subgrant applicant requires updating, you will have to detach the subgrant application from the grant application and request a revision from the subgrant applicant. Revisions are covered in Lesson 13.

Deleting Subgrant Applications

To delete a subgrant application that you have added to your grant application, select the **Delete** link in the **Action** column next to the subgrant application you wish to delete and then confirm the deletion when prompted.

This removes the subgrant application from your grant application. It is still available from the stockpile.

Schedule

The **Schedule** section lists the schedules for each subgrant included in the grant application. To view the schedule details, select the subgrant applicant's name.

Grant applicants are required to enter the total duration for the proposed period of performance. From this section, you may also change the title of your grant application by updating the title of the proposed activity from what was entered when it was created.

Budget

The **Budget** section provides a synopsis of the budgets of all of the subgrant applications included in the grant application. To view budget details, select the subgrant applicant's name. You may also sort the budgets in this section by:

- Cost Classification
- Subgrant Budget Class
- Grant Budget Class
- Project Type

Grant applicants can attach budget narratives and indirect cost rate agreements by clicking on the Attachments button. As a grant applicant, you will find that most of your costs should be in the Contractual and Other categories, unless your agency is performing direct construction.

Properties

The **Properties** section provides a synopsis of the properties of all of the subgrant applications included in the grant application. To view the property details, select the address of the property. You may sort by activity type or subgrant applicant. If none of the attached subgrants propose activities with associated properties, then this will be indicated in this section and no properties will be displayed.

Comments and Attachments

The **Comments and Attachments** section provides a synopsis of all of the comments and attachments in the grant application. You can also add, update and/or delete comments or attachments from this page. When adding comments and attachments, you can select a specific section to which your comment/attachment refers or add them at the application level.

Comments entered in the top section are included in the grant application when it is submitted to FEMA. Comments entered in the bottom section (the **Grant Applicant Review Comments** section) are not included with the grant application when it is submitted to FEMA.

Assurance and Certifications

The **Assurance and Certifications** section provides documents that contain the Federal requirements for all FEMA grants, including the right of the Federal government to review the grant activity. This section is required for grant applicants by FEMA, regardless of whether the applicant enables it for subgrant applications.

Each of the documents must be read carefully, signed, and electronically submitted. If the document is not applicable, grant applicants can select the **Not Applicable** checkbox.

When all of the forms have a complete status, click on the Save and Continue button.

Lesson Summary

In this lesson, you learned about various grant application sections.

Some key points from this lesson:

- Grant applications are completed by the State or Tribal government to apply to FEMA for funding for eligible mitigation activities.
- Grant applicants attach eligible, approved subgrants to their grant application. Subgrant applications cannot be added until they are approved and checked in. Grant as subgrant applications are automatically approved.
- Each subgrant application must be ranked. For PDM grant applications, each application needs to be assigned a unique rank from 1 (highest) to X, where X is the total number of subgrants attached to the grant application.
- For FMA and SRL grant applications, you assign a rank of 1 (high), 2 (medium), or 3 (low) priority to each subgrant application
- The Applicant Information, Contact Information, Comments and Attachments and Assurances and Certifications sections are all similar to the corresponding sections of the grant as subgrant application.
- The Schedule section is a synopsis of all of the schedules of the subgrant applications included in the grant application. Grant applicants are required to enter the total duration for the proposed period of performance.
- The Budget and Properties sections both provide a synopsis of corresponding sections in the subgrant applications attached to the grant application.

Lesson 13: Working with Grant Applications

Lesson Overview

Upon completion of this lesson, you should be able to:

- Update a grant application
- Delete a grant application
- Submit a grant application
- View a submitted grant application
- Revise a submitted grant and subgrant application
- Change a Point of Contact in a submitted grant application

Scenario

State Official: Steve Miller

Community: State of Florida

Problem: Steve has been tasked with creating a grant application that will be sent to FEMA.

Next Step: Steve has created the application; he needs to make a few updates, and give his supervisor Deborah access to sign and submit the application to FEMA.

(Audio Transcript)

Hello. I'm Steve and I work for the State of Florida. I have created a grant application and just need to make a few updates to the information so that it will be ready for my supervisor, Deborah, to sign and submit it to FEMA.

Update Grant Applications

Just as with paper subgrant or grant as subgrant applications, eGrants allows users to create grant applications and return at different times to work on them.

To update a grant application, select the **Work on Un-submitted Grant Application(s)** link from the Grant Applicant Home Page. From the list of un-submitted grant applications, select the **Update Application** link corresponding to the grant application you want to update.

Deleting Grant Applications

Just as with paper-intake subgrant or grant as subgrant applications, eGrants allows users to delete grant applications.

To delete a grant application, select the **Work on Un-submitted Grant Application(s)** link from the Grant Applicant Home Page. From the list of un-submitted grant applications, select the checkbox corresponding to the application you wish to delete, and select the **Delete Application** button.

Providing Access

Remember, Steve does not have Sign/Submit access, so he will need to provide access to the grant application to his supervisor, Deborah. When access to a grant application is provided, it also allows access to the associated award package and quarterly reports, if the grant is approved by FEMA.

Steve has provided Deborah with access to the application for five years to ensure that she will be able to resubmit any grant revisions, and accept the award package, and submit quarterly reports, if the grant is approved by FEMA.

Submitting a Grant Application

Once all of the required fields in each section are completed, the status for that section changes from "Incomplete" to "Complete." Once all of the sections have a status of "Complete," then the application can be signed and sent to FEMA.

Steve does not have Sign/Submit access, so he will need Deborah to sign the application and submit it to FEMA.

The following simulation will illustrate how to submit a Grant Application.

NOTE: Although it is not required that you access and review the contents of any section that is "Complete," it is a good idea to take the time to access these sections and review the information before submitting the grant application.

(Show Me Simulation Transcript)

To begin the Sign/Submit process, from the Grant Applicant Home Page, select the **Work on Un-submitted Grant Application(s)** link.

On the Grant Status: Un-Submitted Grant Applications screen, select the **Update Application** link for the grant application that you wish to submit. For this scenario, select "2012 Florida EMA PDM Grant Application."

All the sections should have a "Complete" status. Select the **Review and Submit Application** link on the Sidebar menu.

The Review and Submit Application screen includes a drop-down for the Federal Fiscal Year. The Fiscal Year is defaulted at the Fiscal Year in which the grant application was created. To change it to reflect the Fiscal Year of the application period for which you are submitting, select the Fiscal Year from the drop-down and then select the **Change Year** button. For this scenario, select "2012".

Begin submitting the application by entering your password into the **Password** field. For security reasons, your Password is not shown in the field. Select the checkbox to certify your electronic signature. Select the **Submit Application** button.

You will receive confirmation that your application has been submitted to FEMA.

Submitted Applications

Once you have submitted a grant application to FEMA, you may monitor its status in eGrants as it is reviewed and approved/disapproved.

To view the status of a submitted grant application, select the **Work on Submitted Grant Application(s)** link on the Grant Applicant Home Page. The Grant Status: Submitted Applications screen is displayed. This screen is split into two parts. At the top of the screen, your pending tasks are listed for the grant applications that you have submitted. This allows you to manage your applications by their Review Status by clicking on the link in the **Action** column.

Below is a list of all of the grant applications you have submitted with the current status of each grant application shown in the **Application Status** column. You can sort the list by Application Year, Application Number or Application Title, or you may select the **Search button** to locate a particular grant application.

Grant Application Review Status

You can review the status of submitted grant applications. The top portion of the Grant Status: Submitted Grant Applications page shows Review Status of Grant Applications. As seen in the image, the Review Status can be: In Progress, Revision Requested, Approved, Awarded, Obligated, and Accepted/Not Accepted.

Review Status

For submitted grant applications that are "In Progress," you can also review the status of the subgrant applications.

In the lower portion of the Grant Status: Submitted Grant Applications page is a list of Grant Applications that have been submitted. Each subgrant attached to a grant, goes through a certain number of reviews. You can view the status of each subgrant that is attached, except for competitive grant programs (PDM & RFC). Select Review Status in the drop-down menu of the grant to which the subgrant you want to review the status of is attached.

For non-competitive grant programs, the **View Status** link in the **Action** column will be active. For non-competitive grant programs, the subgrant Status can be: Pending, Completed, Not Ready, and Rework Requested. For competitive grant programs, you can not view the status of the review of the subgrants, so the **View Status** link in the **Action** column is *NOT* active.

Revisions

Occasionally, FEMA will request that changes be made to a grant application or subgrant application(s) attached to a grant application. eGrants allows the grant applicant to:

- Make FEMA requested revisions to a submitted grant application
- Make FEMA requested revisions to a submitted subgrant application
- Release a subgrant application so that the subgrant applicant can make the FEMA requested revisions

Once all of the requested revisions have been made, the application must be resubmitted to FEMA for further consideration. Only a grant user with Sign/Submit access can resubmit the application.

If a revision is requested by FEMA, an email notifying the grant applicant of the request will be sent to the Authorized Agent and the Point of Contact (POC) provided in the Contact section of the grant application.

Steve has received an email notifying him that there is a revision request on the State of Florida Grant Application he has submitted. Let's help Steve Review the revision request.

NOTE: If you need to revise a grant application that has been submitted to FEMA, FEMA must "release" the application for revision in eGrants. Contact your FEMA regional office to request a revision.

(Show Me Simulation Transcript)

From the Grant Applicant Home Page, select the **Work on Submitted Grant Application(s)** link.

The Grant Status: Submitted Grant Applications screen is displayed. Here you will be able to view the status of any grant applications you have submitted.

Pending tasks for applications and award are showing in the upper portion of the screen and all grant applications you have submitted are shown below.

Select the **Review Revision Requests** link in the **Action** column.

The grant applications for which FEMA has requested a revision are listed.

Locate the grant application you are going to revise.

Select the **Select Action** drop-down menu.

The options in this menu will differ depending on the status of the application. In this scenario, this drop-down menu has 3 options—Review Revision Requests, Edit Contact Information, and Request Revision. Select the "Review Revision Request" item.

Select the **Go** button.

The Overview screen is displayed. All grant revisions requests are shown at the top of the page. Subgrant revision requests are shown at the bottom of the page.

Grant Applicant Revisions

The revision request that Steve has received is for the grant application as well as several sections of one of the subgrant applications attached to the grant application. Steve will be able to make the revisions to the grant application and one of the revisions to the subgrant application, but he will have to get the subgrant applicant to make the remainder of the corrections to the subgrant application.

In the previous simulation, we helped Steve access and review the revision requests. In the following simulations, we will help Steve make the requested revisions by:

- Updating the Schedule section of the grant application
- Updating the Cost Share section of the subgrant application
- Releasing the Cost Estimate section to the subgrant applicant for revisions

First, let's help Steve Update the Schedule section of the grant application.

(Show Me Simulation Transcript)

On the Revision Overview screen, select the **Update** link in the **Action** column for the grant application revision.

An Overview of the grant application is displayed. From here you can access the application section for which FEMA has requested revisions.

In this case, FEMA has requested an update to the Schedule section. Select the **Update** link for the Schedule section.

The section is displayed. From here, you can make the revisions as requested and then save the revisions.

When all of the revisions have been made, you can resubmit the grant application to FEMA for further review.

Grant Applicant Revisions of Subgrant Applications

In the previous simulation, you helped Steve make the requested revisions by updating the grant application. Now, lets help Steve make a revision to one of the subgrant applications.

(Show Me Simulation Transcript)

From the Overview screen, in the subgrant revision requests section, find the subgrant section you are planning on revising.

Review the requested subgrant revisions and comments provided by FEMA. In this case, the comments from FEMA read: "Please revise the Cost Estimate and Update Cost Share to reflect Federal/Non-Federal Cost Share." Select the **Review** link for the revision you are going to work on.

The Review and Resubmit Application screen is displayed.

Select the **Review Section** link for the section you are going to revise. In this case, you are going to make revisions to the Cost Share section.

The Review Cost Share screen is displayed.

In the **Action** column, select the radio button to Update the Cost Share section.

Select the **Save and Continue** button.

The subgrant section you selected, the Cost Share section, is displayed. From here you can make the requested revisions to the application and select the **Save and Continue** button to save your revisions. When all of the revision requests have been completed, you can resubmit the application to FEMA for further review.

Releasing Subgrants for Revisions

In the previous simulations, you helped Steve make the requested revisions by updating the grant application and one section of the subgrant application. Now, lets help Steve release the subgrant application to the subgrant applicant for revision.

(Show Me Simulation Transcript)

From the Overview screen, in the subgrant revision requests section, find the subgrant section you are planning on revising.

Review the requested subgrant revisions and comments provided by FEMA. In this case, the comments from FEMA read: "Please revise the Cost Estimate and Update Cost Share to reflect

Federal/Non-Federal Cost Share." Select the **Review** link for the revision you are going to work on. The Review and Resubmit Application screen is displayed.

Select the **Review Section** link for the section you are going to work on. In this case, you are going to release the Cost Estimate section.

The Review Cost Estimate screen is displayed.

In the **Action** column, select the radio button to Release the Cost Estimate section. Set a revision deadline. In this case, the revision deadline is set for 08-22-2012. Enter comments for the subgrant applicant, if appropriate. In this case, enter "Please revise Cost Estimate section per FEMA request." Select the **Save and Continue** button.

An email is displayed with information that will be emailed to the Authorized Agent and Point of Contact identified in the Contact section of the application. Select the **Release Application Section** button.

You will get a confirmation that the application section was released to the subgrant applicant. Select the **Return to Review and Resubmit** button to return to the list of subgrant revision requests.

You are returned to the Review and Resubmit Application screen.

The status of the Cost Estimate section should now be "Revision Released to Subgrantee."

Resubmitting Revised Applications

Once all of the revisions requested by FEMA have been made, the application will need to be resubmitted to FEMA. The process to resubmit is the same as the Sign/Submit process. Once all of the sections have a status of "Complete," grant applicants with Sign/Submit access can enter in their Passwords, select the Signature checkbox, and select the Resubmit Application button.

Changing the Point of Contact

The Point of Contact (POC) is the person who will receive e-mail messages about the application and the person who will be contacted by FEMA concerning the application, if necessary. The POC information can be changed, if necessary, even after the application has been submitted.

From the **Grant Status: Submitted Grant Applications** screen, select **Edit Contact Information** from the drop-down list in the **Action** column.

NOTE: Both the POC and the alternate POC can be edited.

Lesson Summary

In this lesson, you learned about how to

- Update a grant application
- Delete a grant application
- Submit a grant application
- View a submitted grant application
- Revise a submitted grant and subgrant application
- Change a Point of Contact in a submitted grant application

Some key points from this lesson:

- Grant applications, like paper-intake subgrant applications and grant as subgrant applications, can be created and worked on at different times.
- Grant applications can be signed and submitted by a grant applicant with Sign/Submit access for applications by entering the User's Password and selecting the Signature checkbox.
- Grant Applicants can check the status of submitted grant applications by selecting the **Work on Submitted Grant Application(s)** link.
- FEMA may request a revision to a grant application or subgrant application(s) attached to a grant application. Grant applicants can make the revisions, or request their subgrant applicants to make the revisions for subgrant applications, directly in eGrants and then resubmit the grant application or subgrant application to FEMA.
- Grant applicants can change the POC and alternate POC in a submitted grant application.

Lesson 14: Grant Awards

Lesson Overview

Upon completion of this lesson, you should be able to:

- Review an award package
- Accept an award package
- Not accept an award package
- View a submitted award package
- View a FEMA signed award package

Scenario

State Official: Steve Miller

Community: State of Florida

Problem: Steve has created a grant application and it has been submitted, revised and resubmitted. Steve has received an e-mail stating that the grant application has been approved by FEMA.

Next Step: Steve must review the award package and ensure that his supervisor, Deborah, has access to accept/not accept and sign it.

(Audio Transcript)

Hello. I'm Steve and I work for the State of Florida. I just got an e-mail informing me that the grant application submitted has been approved, and we have an award package that needs to be reviewed, signed, and accepted or not accepted by my supervisor. Let's get started!

Award Packages

When FEMA approves a grant application for award, an e-mail message is sent to the primary and alternate Points of Contact (POC) provided in the grant application, notifying them that there is an award package for review in eGrants.

The award package has three parts:

- Award Letter
- Agreement Articles
- Obligating Document for Award/Amendment (FEMA Form 76-10a)

The package must be reviewed, accepted or not accepted, and signed.

NOTE: Remember, only users with Sign/Submit access for award packages in eGrants may accept/not accept and sign a grant award package.

Reviewing an Award Package

The award package is listed in eGrants with an "Approved" status in the Awards section of the pending tasks table on the Grant Status: Submitted Grant Applications screen.

Steve has received an e-mail informing him that his grant application has been approved and that there is an award package pending review.

(Show Me Simulation Transcript)

The award packages are shown in the Awards section of the Grant Status: Submitted Grant Applications screen. Select the **Review Award Package(s)** link in the **Action** column.

The applications that have award packages are listed. Select the drop-down menu in the **Action** column for the application you wish to review. This menu has 2 options – Review Award Package and Request revision. Select the "Review Award Package" item.

Select the **Go** button next to the drop-down menu.

The Award Package Overview screen is displayed. From this screen, you can begin reviewing the package either by using the **Review Award Package(s)** link in the Sidebar menu on the left or selecting the **Continue** button. For this scenario, select the **Review Award Package(s)** link in the Sidebar menu.

Select the **Review Package** link to display the Review Award Package screen, which allows grantees to view the award package. The three parts of the award package are displayed. You can navigate to each of the parts by selecting the link.

The Review Award Package Screen

In addition to using the **Review Award Package** screen to access the three parts of the award package, grant applicants can print copies of the award package by selecting the **Print Award Package** button.

The grant applicant can view any of the subgrant applications that were included in the grant application by selecting the **Application Number** link. The grant applicant can also view the cost estimate for any of the subgrant applications that were included in the grant application by selecting the **View Details** link in the Revised Cost column.

Accepting an Award Package

Once you have reviewed the award package, you must either accept or not accept the award. To accept an award package in eGrants, the user must have Sign/Submit access for award packages.

Deborah is going to accept and sign the award package.

(Show Me Simulation Transcript)

On the Review Award Package screen, select the **Accepted** radio button located under the Award Status section.

Scroll down and enter your password in the **Password** field. For this scenario, enter "florida1." Select the **Signature** checkbox. Select the **Save and Continue** button.

Once you have signed and accepted the award package, you will have to wait for FEMA to obligate the award.

(Audio Transcript)

Hi, I am Deborah, Steve's supervisor. Since Steve does not have Sign/Submit access in eGrants, he provided me with access to the grant application for five years. I will need to accept and sign the award package.

Not Accepting an Award Package

Grant applicants may choose not to accept award packages for a variety of reasons, including:

- The project is no longer appropriate
- The matching funds are not available
- Funding was secured through other means

The process of not accepting an award package is like the process of accepting it. You must review the award package, select the **Not Accepted radio button**, provide comments, enter the Passwords, select the **Signature** checkbox, and select the **Save and Continue button**.

NOTE: To not accept an award, the user must have Sign/Submit access for award packages in eGrants.

Signed Award Packages

Once you have accepted an award package, the status becomes "Accepted" and is sent to FEMA for finalization. Once FEMA has "signed" the award package, the status will change to "Awarded." The funds are not available until the status of the award package is "Obligated."

Viewing Signed Award Packages

You may view award packages with an "Accepted" or "Not Accepted" status. You may also view FEMA signed award packages with a status of "Awarded" or "Obligated." The award package is read-only and cannot be modified in any way.

Steve wants to view the award package that Deborah has accepted.

(Show Me Simulation Transcript)

In the pending tasks section of the Grant Status: Submitted Grant Applications screen (upper section), select the **View Award Package(s)** link.

Select the drop-down menu in the **Action** column for the application that you would like to review. This drop-down menu has three options – View Award Package, Edit Contact Information, and Request revision. Select the "View Award Package" item. Select the **Go** button.

Select the **View Award Package(s)** link in the Sidebar menu or the **Continue** button.

Select the **View Package** link in the **Action** column.

The View Award Package screen is displayed. From here, you can view each part of the package by selecting the corresponding link.

Lesson Summary

In this lesson, you learned about various aspects of an award package.

Some key points from this lesson:

- Award packages can be reviewed directly in eGrants and accepted or not accepted.
- The award package contains three parts-the award letter, the agreement articles, and the obligating document for award/amendment (FEMA Form 76-10a).
- Award packages are shown in the Awards section of the Grant Status: Submitted Grant Applications screen.
- You can print a copy of the award package.
- Award packages accepted or not accepted by the grant applicant but not yet finalized by FEMA have a status of "Accepted" or "Not Accepted" and can be viewed as read-only. FEMA-signed award packages have a status of "Awarded" or "Obligated" and can also be viewed at any time as read-only.

Lesson 15: Quarterly Reports

Lesson Overview

Upon completion of this lesson, you should be able to:

- Describe the types of quarterly reports
- Prepare a quarterly report
- Update a quarterly report
- Sign a quarterly report
- Submit a quarterly report
- Review a quarterly report
- Revise a submitted quarterly report
- Resubmit a revised quarterly report

Scenario

State Official: Steve Miller

Community: State of Florida

Problem: Steve has created a grant application, which was submitted, and awarded by FEMA.

Next Step: Several months have passed and now Steve needs to complete a quarterly report for the grant in eGrants.

(Audio Transcript)

Hello. I'm Steve and I work for the State of Florida. We received a grant award from FEMA several months ago and have been monitoring our subgrant awards. Now it's time for me to begin working on the quarterly reports that are due to FEMA.

Quarterly Reports

FEMA requires that grantees report quarterly on the performance and financial status of grants that have been awarded. The reports are due to FEMA no later than 30 days after the end of each Federal fiscal quarter following the award date.

eGrants allows you to prepare and submit these reports through the Quarterly Reports function. The Quarterly Reports function is activated for a grant when FEMA finalizes the grant. Once a grant is obligated by FEMA, you can access the first quarterly report to complete and submit to FEMA. On the first day of each quarter thereafter, the next quarterly report that is due is activated in the quarterly reports list until the grant performance period has expired.

Financial and Performance Quarterly Reports

Grantees may report on the status of their subgrants individually or as a whole:

- Performance Reports
    - Subgrant Quarterly Performance Reports
    - Grantee Quarterly Performance Reports
- Financial Status Reports
    - Subgrant Quarterly Financial Status Reports
    - Grantee Quarterly Financial Status Report

NOTE: Currently, there is no quarterly report function for subgrantees to submit performance or financial status reports via eGrants. Therefore, grantees may want to record the status of subgrants in the Subgrant Quarterly Reports.

NOTE: Beginning in 2009, Grantees are **_required_** to submit Grantee Quarterly Performance and Financial Status Reports electronically through eGrants.

Preparing a Quarterly Report

The quarterly reports function will show a list of the quarterly reports for the applicable grant, the status of each report, and the deadline to submit each report. The status for a report can be one of the following:

- Incomplete-not ready to be submitted to FEMA
- Complete-ready to be signed and/or submitted to FEMA
- Submitted to FEMA-already submitted to FEMA; lists the date it was submitted
- Revision Requested by FEMA-submitted and returned by FEMA for revision; lists the date the revision was requested
- Revision Submitted to FEMA - resubmitted with revisions to FEMA; lists the date it was resubmitted

(Show Me Simulation Transcript)

From the Grant Applicant Home Page, select the **Work on Submitted Grant Application(s)** link.

Select the drop-down menu for the grant application for which you want to prepare the quarterly report. This drop-down menu has four options – Review Revision Requests, Review Award Package, Manage Grant, and Request revision. Select the "Manage Grant" item. Select the **Go** button.

On the Quarterly Reports screen, you will see all of the available quarterly reports and the status of each. Select the **Update** link in the **Action** column for the quarterly report you want to prepare.

To begin working on each section of the quarterly reports select the **Incomplete** link in the **Action** column.

Working on the Quarterly Reports

Once you have selected the quarterly report you want to work on, you will see that there are four forms that can be completed: Two are performance reports (one subgrant report, one grantee report), and two are financial status reports (one subgrant report, one grantee report).

If a grantee chooses not to submit individual status reports for his or her subgrants, he or she may select the **Not Electronically Submitted (NES)** checkbox in the Actioncolumn for Subgrant Quarterly Performance Reports and/or Subgrant Quarterly Financial Reports. The status of reports will change to "NES" once the **Save** or **Save and Continue** button is selected.

Updating a Quarterly Report

Just like completing applications, eGrants allows you to begin a quarterly report and return at a later time to continue working on it. Until all of the required fields have been completed or the **Not Electronically Submitted (NES)** checkbox has been selected, the status of the report is "Incomplete." Once you have completed all of the required sections or checked the **Not Electronically Submitted (NES)** check box, the status becomes "Complete."

Steve has already started the grantee quarterly performance report. He has been told by his supervisor that the Subgrant Quarterly Performance Reports will not be electronically submitted this quarter. The Grantee Quarterly Financial Status Report has been completed by the Financial team.

Let's help Steve complete the quarterly report package.

(Show Me Simulation Transcript)

Steve has already completed the Grantee Quarterly Performance Report.

From the Update Quarterly Report screen, select the **NES** check box for the Subgrant Quarterly Performance Report.

Select the **Save and Continue** button.

Signing a Quarterly Report

Once both of the report forms in either the Performance Report or the Financial Status Report have a status of either "Complete" or "NES," the quarterly reports can be signed. A user must have Sign/Submit access for Performance Reports to sign them and Sign/Submit access for Financial Reports to sign them.

Steve has completed the Quarterly Performance Report, and the financial office has completed the Quarterly Financial Report so the entire quarterly report package is "Complete." Help Deborah sign the quarterly reports.

The following simulation will illustrate how to sign the quarterly reports. To begin the simulation, select the Launch Simulation button. For the text alternative, select the link below.

NOTE: A user must have Sign/Submit access for Performance Reports to sign them; Sign/Submit access for Financial Reports to sign them; and Sign/Submit access for Quarterly Report Packages to sign and submit them to FEMA.

NOTE: If changes are made to the quarterly report after it has been signed (but before it has been submitted to FEMA), then it will need to be signed again.

(Audio Transcript)

Hi, I'm Deborah, Steve's supervisor. Steve has completed the quarterly reports, but since he does not have Sign/Submit access, I will need to sign the quarterly reports.

(Show Me Simulation Transcript)

Access the quarterly report you are submitting by selecting the **Update** link in the **Action** column on the Quarterly Reports screen.

Select the **Password** field.

Enter your password. In this case, its "grantapp."

Select the **Signature** check box.

Select the **Submit Performance Report** button.

You will receive a confirmation that the quarterly report has been submitted.

Submitting Quarterly Report Packages

Once both the Quarterly Performance Report and the Quarterly Financial Status Report are complete and signed, the Quarterly Report package can be submitted to FEMA. Only an ***entire*** Quarterly Report package can be submitted to FEMA, including a completed and signed Quarterly Performance report as well as a completed and signed Quarterly Financial Status Report. A user must have Sign/Submit access for Quarterly Report packages to sign and submit the package to FEMA.

Help Deborah submit the Quarterly Report package to FEMA.

(Audio Transcript)

Hi, I'm Deborah, Steve's supervisor. Steve has completed the quarterly reports, but since he does not have Sign/Submit access, I have signed them. Now I will need to sign and submit the entire quarterly report package to FEMA.

Revising Submitted Quarterly Reports

You can view quarterly reports that have been submitted to FEMA. You may also revise a quarterly report that you have previously submitted. If there is an error in a quarterly report, the grantee can request that FEMA release the quarterly performance and/or financial status report(s) to make a revision or FEMA can initiate a request for revision to a quarterly performance and/or financial status report(s).

Resubmitting Quarterly Reports

Once the changes/revisions have been made to the quarterly report(s), a grant applicant user with Sign/Submit access will need to sign the revised quarterly report(s). The process is the same as for the original quarterly report. Once both the Quarterly Performance Report and Quarterly Financial Status Report have been signed, the entire Quarterly Report package can be signed and resubmitted to FEMA.

Enter your password in the **Password** field. Select the **electronic signature** check box for the Quarterly Report. Select the **Save and Continue** button.

Lesson Summary

- In this lesson, you learned about various aspects of quarterly reports.

  Some key points from this lesson:

  - FEMA requires that grantees report quarterly on the performance and financial status of grants that have been awarded.
  - The reports are due to FEMA no later than 30 days after the end of each Federal fiscal quarter following the award date.
  - The Subgrant Quarterly Performance Report and Subgrant and Grantee Financial Status Reports can be submitted via paper and indicated as Not Electronically Submitted in the quarterly report package.

  NOTE: Beginning in 2009, Grantees are required to submit Grantee Quarterly Performance and Financial Status Reports electronically through eGrants.

  - A user must have Sign/Submit access for Performance Reports to sign them; Sign/Submit access for Financial Status Reports to sign them; and Sign/Submit access for Quarterly Report Packages to sign and submit them to FEMA.

- If there is an error in a submitted quarterly report or you find that some information has changed, you can request that FEMA release the report back to you to make a revision or FEMA can request that you make a revision to a quarterly report.

You have completed IS-31: Mitigation eGrants for the Grant Applicant.